Norma Miller is a successful food writer and author of many
other titles, including:

Slow Cooking: Best New Recipes
The Halogen Oven Cookbook
One-Pot Dishes for Every Season
The Food Mixer Cookbook
The Sous Vide Recipe Book
Waffles, Crepes and Pancakes
Soups: Simple and easy recipes for soup-making machines

Superfood Soups

Norma Miller

....

A How To Book

ROBINSON

ROBINSON

First published in Great Britain in 2016 by Robinson

Copyright © Norma Miller, 2016

1 3 5 7 9 10 8 6 4 2

The moral right of the authors has been asserted.

IMPORTANT NOTE
The recommendations in this book are solely intended as education and information and should not be taken as medical advice.

A CIP catalogue record for this book is available from the British Library.

ISBN: 978-1-47213-883-5

Typeset by Basement Press, Glaisdale
Printed and bound in Great Britain by CPI Group (UK) Ltd, Croydon CR0 4YY

Papers used by Robinson are from well-managed forests and other responsible sources.

MIX
Paper from
responsible sources
FSC
www.fsc.org   FSC® C104740

Robinson
is an imprint of
Little, Brown Book Group
Carmelite House
50 Victoria Embankment
London EC4Y 0DZ

An Hachette UK Company
www.hachette.co.uk

www.littlebrown.co.uk

How To Books are published by Robinson, an imprint of Little, Brown Book Group. We welcome proposals from authors who have first-hand experience of their subjects. Please set out the aims of your book, its target market and its suggested contents in an email to Nikki.Read@howtobooks.co.uk.

Contents

Introduction

Home-made soups are more popular than ever and superfoods are all the rage. So what could be better than superfood soups? Superfoods are all about using as wide a range as possible of good quality, fresh ingredients in your cooking. Superfoods mean creating delicious, satisfying meals – food you will really want to eat, and food you will go on making and enjoying over and over again. The recipes in this book for superfood soups will help to make it easy and delicious for you to eat well and sustainably for long-term health benefits.

SOUPS AND SUPERFOODS

It's important for all of us to review our lifestyle choices from time to time. What we eat is obviously a big part of this and the ideas which have arisen in connection with superfoods point the way to better health and more fulfilment. Superfoods are all about using as wide a range as possible of good quality fresh ingredients in your cooking. Many types of superfoods are all around us and familiar from our everyday cooking and eating. We eat them already without giving them a second thought. Some superfoods I've used in my recipes may be less familiar, but there is no need to aim for weird and extraordinary ingredients.

Try to forget about any types of food that are widely regarded as unhealthy. There's always plenty of advice about the latest research and official health warnings to be found online and in newspapers, but endeavour to avoid faddishness, don't go to extremes, and don't rely on claims for any single 'miracle' food.

Before You Start

- Gather together and prepare all the ingredients you will need before you start to cook.
- For best results cut ingredients into thin slices or 2.5cm (1in) dice.
- Never overfill the soup maker: the maximum capacity for the total volume of ingredients is marked on the machine and is to be found in the instruction booklet which comes with the appliance.
- In the case of the jug-style soup maker, there is a minimum marker in the jug. Your ingredients and liquid must go above this minimum marker to ensure that the blades work correctly.
- The recipes are a guide; machines vary both in motor speed and functions, and vegetables and fruits are never standard in shape and size.
- When in use, the surfaces of the machine will become very hot.
- To prevent damage to the motor it is important to use the blend function continuously only for the time mentioned in the handbook for your particular machine. It may be as little as one minute for one particular model or three minutes for another. Allow the machine to cool before using the blend function again.
- Always let the machine cool before making a second batch of soup.
- Soup is only as good as the quality of the ingredients, especially the stock. Make your own with the recipes in this book or use the best quality available that is full of flavour but low in salt.

Instead, opt for nutritional variety, look for good quality, fresh ingredients, and always aim to make colourful, appealing and appetising meals. Eating can and should be one of life's great pleasures, indispensable in support of health and happiness.

This brings me back to soups. Your soup maker is the optimal way of harnessing the goodness in superfoods, as it seals them all in throughout the cooking process. There's an amazing world of tasty and nutritious soups to explore, and I hope you will share my enthusiasm for soups and superfoods by trying out my recipes.

There is something immensely enjoyable and satisfying about sitting down to a bowl of delicious home-made soup. To help you along, always maintain a good stock of spices and store-cupboard essentials, be sure to have top quality fresh ingredients to hand, and always keep your soup maker at the ready.

Easy superfoods to start with are the colourful vegetables, such as tomatoes, sweet potatoes, rainbow coloured chard, almost black cavolo nero, broccoli, red cabbage and spinach, as well as the essential onions and garlic. Colourful fruits too, like plums, cherries, blackberries, raspberries, blueberries and redcurrants when in season. Then there are all the fresh leafy herbs and the spices, such as turmeric, chilli and cinnamon. And don't forget nuts and seeds, including walnuts and almonds, pumpkin seeds, sunflower seeds and pine nuts. Make a point of choosing healthy, lean meats, poultry and game. Go for oily fish, such as salmon or mackerel, as well as white fish and shellfish. Soups are a great way to get these super ingredients into your diet. You can't help making a nutrient-rich, healthy soup if you follow the recipes and use the ingredients to be found in this book. You'll get all the vitamins, minerals, protein and other essentials for wellbeing if you eat these soups regularly and often.

THE SOUP MAKER - WHAT IS IT?

A soup maker is a portable, free-standing electric appliance which cooks and blends ingredients to make a soup to the consistency of your choice: chunky or smooth. There are two types of machines available on the market – a blender-style soup maker and a jug-style soup maker. Each type of machine works slightly differently. Throughout the book I've referred to the blender-style soup maker as having a glass jar in which the ingredients are put and the jug-style soup maker as having a metal jug.

Blender-style Soup Maker

This type of soup maker looks rather like a conventional blender, but is heavier. These machines are more expensive than the jug-style machines, but they do have extra features and functions which give greater flexibility. With no pre-programmed settings to cook and blend the raw ingredients you are in full control of the whole process, whether browning onions, deciding how long you simmer the soup for, or adding extra ingredients part way through. Even noodles, pasta, pulses and grains can be added later in the process to heat through because they won't be blended to a pulp.

This soup maker consists of a glass jar section which is a complete unit: the glass jar, a handle, a non-stick cooking plate and a collar with blades. The assembly sits on the powerful motor base, where the simple-to-use controls are located. The blending control dial lets you choose between several different settings from low to high speed as well as a pulse setting, so there is plenty of control over how chunky or smooth the soup will be. For safety, the blending control only works when the cooking or heating process has completed.

The stir button is useful as it can be used at any time, while onions are frying or just to mix the ingredients together when they all go into the glass jar. The timer control can be adjusted from one to thirty minutes. If at the end of the thirty minutes cooking time the meat or vegetables aren't tender, just reset the timer for another 10–15 minutes. Heat or temperature controls will start the cooking cycle. Select from either high, low or simmer. The temperature can be changed at any time during the heating or cooking cycle.

Some machines have additional functions; they can be used as a traditional blender, make smoothies, mix cold ingredients and crush ice. A great function of this machine, especially for soup making, is that ingredients such as onions and garlic can be browned, fried or sautéed in a little oil and butter (poured or dropped onto the cooking plate rather than the blades) in the base of the machine, adding colour and great flavour. The glass jar lets you see the food cooking, which is an advantage, as it gives you a window onto what's happening throughout the cooking process. The lid has a removable measuring cup which must be in place when the soup is cooking and blending. It is normal for steam to escape around the measuring cup, so handle it with care, as it will be hot. Soups bubble up during cooking, so the maximum fill level for blending hot ingredients is less than for blending cold ingredients, and both are marked on the side of the glass jar.

Extra ingredients which need little cooking can be added part way through the cooking process; either stop the machine, or reduce the temperature to simmer. Using oven gloves, carefully remove the measuring cup and wait until the built-up steam disperses (to avoid scalding). Carefully add the ingredients and replace the measuring cup; restart the machine and continue cooking.

Raw fish, poultry or meat and frozen vegetables and fruits can be used in this type of soup maker.

Jug-style Soup Maker

This type of soup maker looks rather like a large, metal, lidded jug, but is heavier. The lid is the motor unit with built-in blender blades and an overfill sensor. A plastic measuring jug is a useful extra. Soups bubble up during cooking, so the maximum fill level is marked on the side of the metal jug. There is also a minimum level because the blades have to reach the ingredients. Always make sure that your ingredients are between the minimum and maximum marks on the jug before you start cooking: it can damage the motor if run empty or below the minimum level. Stock or water can be added to savoury soups and unsweetened fruit juice to sweet ones to increase the total quantity in the jug without altering the other ingredients. The jug is metal not glass so it's essential to check the levels each time you cook – it's not possible to check with a glance at the machine during cooking.

The jug-style soup maker is very simple and easy to use as it has two automatic pre-programmed soup settings to cook and blend ingredients: purée or chunky, and just one other function button to operate the machine – the blend/clean setting. Unlike the blender-style models, this style of machine does not have a function for browning onions. For safety, the blending control only works when the cooking or heating process has completed. To prevent damage to the motor it is important to use the blend function continuously only for the time mentioned in the handbook for your particular machine. It may be as little as one minute for one particular model or three minutes for another. Allow the machine to cool before using the blend function again.

Never start the machine when it is empty and always let it cool before making a second batch of soup. Some food cannot be used in this type of soup maker. Do not use raw meat, poultry, game or fish and shellfish. Do not use cooked, frozen meat, poultry, game or fish and shellfish which haven't been completely thawed. Let frozen vegetables and fruits thaw before use, too.

Jug-style Soup Maker Cooking Settings

Option 1: Purée. Put the ingredients into the metal jug and fit the lid in place. Press the purée button and the soup maker is automatically programmed to heat and blend the soup. This takes about 20–25 minutes.

Option 2: Chunky. Put the ingredients into the metal jug and fit the lid in place. Select and press the chunky button and the soup maker is automatically programmed to heat the soup (this option is not programmed to automatically blend the soup). This takes about 30 minutes. At this stage you can carefully lift the lid and add any final ingredients such as chopped fresh herbs or cream. Replace the lid and press the blend/clean button, if necessary, to alter the consistency.

Care and Cleaning

Always unplug your machine and let it cool before cleaning. If the machine has a 'self-cleaning' feature; just follow the manufacturer's instructions. If you need to clean your machine by hand, take care to avoid touching the blades, which are very sharp. Do not clean the machine or accessories in a dishwasher; depending on the type of machine, the inside of the glass jar or metal jug can be cleaned with hot soapy water and the outside wiped with a damp cloth. Never immerse the machine, power cord or electric plug in hot water.

Adapting Your Own Recipes for the Soup Maker

You probably have several favourite soup recipes that you'd usually cook on the hob or in a microwave oven. Many of these may be suitable to adapt to make in the soup maker; you just need to experiment a little. Bear in mind the manufacturer's guidelines for using your particular soup maker, such as whether or not ingredients can go into the machine raw or frozen. Often it's just a matter of letting the frozen vegetables or fruits thaw and using cooked meat, poultry, game and fish or shellfish in place of raw.

All soup makers have a maximum capacity for the total volume of all the liquids and the prepared ingredients. As a rough guide, I add up all the liquid quantities – the stock, water, tomato juice, passata or yogurt in the recipe – and if this is around 700ml (1¼

Important Safety Advice

This advice is common sense when using any kitchen appliance.
- The soup maker must be on a stable, heat-proof surface and not near the edge of work surfaces.
- Keep the surrounding areas clear, ensuring there is adequate space around the soup maker for air to circulate.
- Only use the soup maker indoors.
- Don't move the machine when in use and don't leave it unattended.
- Don't use the appliance when empty.
- The blades are extremely sharp so don't put your hands on them.
- Before starting to cook in the soup maker, make sure the lid is securely on top of the machine.
- Keep children and pets away from the soup maker when in use.
- Don't immerse the machine, power cord or electric plug in hot water or place in a dishwasher.
- Leave the machine to cool down completely before putting away.
- If any faults occur with your soup maker, always contact the manufacturer.

pints) then with the other chopped ingredients added, the total ingredients should fit into your soup maker. If the quantities are too large for your machine then reduce everything by a quarter, a third or a half, as required. When reducing quantities, remember to reduce the spices and herbs as well.

You can of course cook the recipes from this book conventionally on the hob or in the microwave oven. On the hob, brown the vegetables, meat or fish in a little oil before adding the remaining ingredients. Bring to the boil, reduce the heat and simmer until cooked. If using a microwave oven, cook the soup in two to three batches. Big quantities and cold liquids can, surprisingly, take longer to cook in a microwave than on the hob and some microwaves have small capacities.

About the Ingredients

I like looking out for good quality, fresh ingredients whether it's in a local store, on visiting farmers' markets or at the supermarket and using what I can find to inspire me in my choice of what to cook. For these recipes I have used a mixture of fresh seasonal produce, store-cupboard ingredients, vacuum packed foods and canned foods, as well as some frozen items. By using your soup maker and putting in the ingredients yourself, you know exactly what you are eating and can be sure of the quality and provenance of the ingredients, too.

Tips for Using a Soup Maker

- Never leave the machine unattended when it is in use.
- For best results cut most foods into even-sized thin slices or 2.5cm (1in) dice to ensure they cook evenly.
- As soup makers are sealed units, liquid doesn't evaporate during the cooking process, and doesn't therefore concentrate the flavours as happens in a saucepan on the hob, so always taste for seasoning before serving and adjust as necessary.
- The blender-style machines have a useful measuring cup in the lid for tipping extra ingredients into the machine during the cooking process. After use, always replace securely in the main lid as the hot liquid could splash out of the machine.
- For machines with a browning or frying function, pour a little oil or butter onto the blades before adding the onions to soften – this will prevent them sticking.
- For machines without a browning function, prepared ingredients can be sautéed in a hot frying pan with a little oil until golden before adding to the machine.
- If the soup is too thick, thin it with a little boiling water poured from the kettle.
- Ready-cooked rice, noodles, pasta, grains and pulses can be heated in a microwave oven until piping hot to be stirred immediately into bowls of soup.

Soup maker soups are speedy, so I make use of quickly cooked additions to stir into the soup or serve on the side, such as fresh pasta and noodles or sachets of pre-cooked varieties of rice, pulses, grains and noodles.

My store-cupboard always contains a wide selection of seeds, nuts, spices and spice mixes, ready-to-eat dried fruits and small jars of pastes and purées that are so quick and convenient, but have a big impact on the flavour of your cooking. I try to avoid excess salt and sugar in my recipes; if you prefer you can always add a little, but use with discretion and always taste the food before you add anything – you might surprise yourself and not need it at all, particularly if you pack your food with flavour from really good ingredients and added herbs and spices.

The basis of a great soup is a really good stock. I've included five recipes for stock in the chapter on extras. If you buy stock, make sure it's very good quality, whether granules, concentrated liquids or ready-prepared varieties, and that the salt levels aren't high.

About the Recipes

The recipes in this book are easy to follow and uncomplicated. They are also a guide, and don't need to be taken literally: machines vary, and vegetables and fruits are never standard in shape and size. Don't worry if your courgettes are a few grams underweight or if you're not sure whether your handful of basil leaves is too big or too small.

The recipes take into account the differences between the two types of machine. The main steps for each recipe give instructions for the blender-style soup maker. If you have a jug-style soup maker, follow the alternative instructions given at the end of the recipe. All the recipes have been designed for cooking in a soup maker, and the preparation and cooking processes for each recipe are straightforward and easy to follow.

In many of the recipes I've used the vegetables and other ingredients to thicken the soups. If after trying a recipe you would prefer a thicker soup the next time you make it, just add a little flour or cornflour blended to a paste with water. The recipes are often adaptable, and you can easily substitute inter-changeable ingredients of your choice the next time you cook a dish, as long as they don't exceed the capacity of the machine. If you are preparing food for someone who has a food allergy, be sure to study the list of ingredients carefully and make the necessary substitutions before you begin.

Throughout the book there are plenty of serving suggestions and hints and tips to go with the recipes. Mostly the recipes make four servings, but they will serve more or less, depending on appetites and whether they are eaten as a snack, a starter, a main meal or supper.

For convenience, the recipe ingredients are listed in the order in which they are used. Though they are given in imperial as well as metric, you will find the metric measurements easier. All spoon measures are level unless otherwise stated.

Roots, Tubers and Bulbs

From the goodness of the soil come the earth's underground treasures. Roots, tubers and bulbs are true superfoods, ideally suited to making wonderful, nourishing soups. With forceful and unmistakable flavours, these soups are richly earthy and smooth with peppery overtones and more than a hint of sweetness. They are perfect for winter days and cold snaps, or for warmth, comfort and a surge of energy at any other time.

Beetroot Soup with Tamarind and Yogurt

Tamarind paste gives a sweet and sour taste to the beetroots.

SERVES 4
1 medium red onion
6 medium-sized cooked beetroots (not in vinegar)
1 small orange
2 tbsp sunflower oil
Small handful of parsley leaves
1 tbsp tamarind paste
700ml (1¼ pints) chicken or vegetable stock
Freshly milled black pepper, to taste
150ml (¼ pint) natural Greek yogurt
Natural Greek yogurt and a few parsley leaves, to serve

1   Finely chop the onion and cut the beetroots into small cubes. Finely grate the zest of half the orange, cut in half and squeeze out the juice.
2   Put the oil into the glass jar. Set the timer to 30 minutes and the temperature to high. Add the onion, cover and cook for 1–2 minutes until starting to soften. Use the stir button occasionally.
3   Add the remaining ingredients except the yogurt, cover, stir to mix and bring to the boil for 2–3 minutes, then reduce the heat to simmer and cook for the remaining time using the stir button occasionally. Blend to the consistency you prefer. Add the yogurt, cover and stir for a few seconds without boiling. Season to taste, if necessary.
4   Ladle or pour the piping hot soup into bowls, top with a swirl of yogurt and a few parsley leaves and serve immediately.

JUG-STYLE SOUP MAKER
Put all the prepared ingredients (step 1 above) and other ingredients except the yogurt into the metal jug. Secure the lid in place. Select the purée function and leave to cook. Add the yogurt, replace the lid and blend for a second. Season to taste, if necessary. Serve the soup as in step 4 above.

Spiced Sweet Potato and Coriander Soup

Sweet potato, with its warm orangey colour, gives a hint of sweetness and a silky-smooth texture.

SERVES 4
1 large onion
2 garlic cloves
2 red chillies
500g (1lb 2oz) sweet potatoes
Small bunch of coriander leaves
2 tbsp olive oil
1 tsp ground cumin
1 tsp ground coriander
700ml (1¼ pints) vegetable or chicken stock
Freshly milled black pepper, to taste
Olive oil and finely chopped coriander leaves, to serve

1   Finely chop the onion and crush the garlic. Cut the chillies in half, remove the stalks and seeds and thinly slice. Cut the sweet potatoes into small pieces. Pull the coriander leaves from the stalks.
2   Put the oil into the glass jar. Set the timer to 30 minutes and the temperature to high. Add the onion and garlic, cover and cook for 1–2 minutes using the stir button occasionally. Add the sweet potato, cover and cook for 3–5 minutes until steaming, using the stir button occasionally.
3   Add the remaining ingredients, cover, stir to mix and bring to the boil for 2–3 minutes, then reduce the heat to simmer and cook for the remaining time using the stir button occasionally. Blend to the consistency you prefer. Season to taste, if necessary.
4   Ladle or pour the piping hot soup into bowls. Serve immediately, with a little oil drizzled over and a sprinkling of chopped coriander.

JUG-STYLE SOUP MAKER
Put all the prepared ingredients (step 1 above) and other ingredients into the metal jug. Secure the lid in place. Select the chunky function and leave to cook. Blend to the consistency you prefer and season to taste, if necessary. Serve the soup as in step 4 above.

Curried Onion Soup

Three different types of onion are used in this soup to give it a fuller flavour.

SERVES 4
1 large Spanish onion
2 red onions
4 shallots
2 garlic cloves
2 tbsp olive oil
700ml (1¼ pints) vegetable, mushroom or chicken stock
Small handful of parsley leaves
1 tbsp curry paste, choose your favourite strength
1 tsp ground cumin
1 tsp garam masala
Pinch of salt
Freshly milled black pepper, to taste
Mango chutney, grated cucumber, yogurt and hot naan bread,
   to serve

1   Thinly slice the onions and shallots, and crush the garlic.
2   Put the oil into the glass jar. Set the timer to 30 minutes and the temperature to high. Add the onion, shallots and garlic, cover and cook for 6–8 minutes using the stir button occasionally.
3   Add the remaining ingredients, cover, stir to mix and bring to the boil for 4–5 minutes, then reduce the heat to simmer and cook for the remaining time using the stir button occasionally. Season to taste, if necessary.
4   Ladle or pour the piping hot soup into bowls. Serve immediately with mango chutney, grated cucumber, yogurt and hot naan bread on the side.

JUG-STYLE SOUP MAKER
Put all the prepared ingredients (step 1 above) and other ingredients into the metal jug. Secure the lid in place. Select the chunky function and leave to cook. Season to taste, if necessary. Serve the soup as in step 4 above.

Mooli, Mushroom and Pasta Soup

Mooli is a large white radish with a mild peppery taste. Use radishes instead if you cannot find mooli.

SERVES 4
4 spring onions
1 garlic clove
1 mooli, about 250g (9oz) or 2 bunches of red radishes
400g (14oz) chestnut mushrooms
2.5cm (1in) piece of fresh root ginger
2 tbsp olive oil
700ml (1¼ pints) vegetable, mushroom or chicken stock
200g (7oz) fresh pasta shapes
Freshly milled black pepper, to taste

1   Thinly slice the spring onions and crush the garlic. Chop the mooli into small pieces. If using radishes, trim off the roots and stalks and slice. Roughly chop the mushrooms and grate the ginger.
2   Put the oil into the glass jar. Set the timer to 20 minutes and the temperature to high. Add the spring onions, garlic and mushrooms, cover and cook for 2–3 minutes using the stir button occasionally. Add the mooli or radishes, cover and cook for 3–5 minutes until steaming, using the stir button occasionally.
3   Add the remaining ingredients except the pasta, cover, stir to mix and bring to the boil for 2 minutes. Reduce the heat to simmer and cook for the remaining time using the stir button occasionally.
4   While the soup is cooking, cook the pasta following the packet instructions.
5   Blend to the consistency you prefer. Stir the piping hot pasta into the soup. Season to taste, if necessary.
6   Ladle or pour the piping hot soup into bowls. Serve immediately.

JUG-STYLE SOUP MAKER
Put all the prepared ingredients (step 1 above) and other ingredients except the pasta into the metal jug. Secure the lid in place. Select the chunky function and leave to cook. To cook the pasta follow step 4 above. Blend to the consistency you prefer. Season to taste, if necessary. Serve with the pasta as in steps 5 and 6 above.

Jerusalem Artichoke Soup

Jerusalem Artichokes have a knobbly skin and a nutty taste.

SERVES 4

2 tbsp lemon juice
400g (14oz) Jerusalem artichokes
4 shallots
2 garlic cloves
Small bunch of chives
2 tbsp olive oil
150ml (¼ pint) milk
700ml (1¼ pints) vegetable or chicken stock
Freshly milled white pepper
4 tbsp single cream
Chopped chives and hot crusty bread, to serve

1   Pour the lemon juice into a bowl of cold water. Scrub the
    Jerusalem artichokes to remove any soil. I like to leave the skins
    on, but scrape or peel the skin if you prefer. Roughly chop and
    put them in the lemon water to prevent browning. Finely chop
    the shallots and crush the garlic. Snip the chives with scissors.
2   Put the oil into the glass jar. Set the timer to 30 minutes and the
    temperature to high. Add the shallots and garlic, cover and cook
    for 1–2 minutes until softened using the stir button occasionally.
    Add the drained Jerusalem artichokes, cover and cook for 3–4
    minutes until steaming using the stir button occasionally.

3 Add the remaining ingredients except the cream, cover, stir to mix and bring to the boil for 2–3 minutes. Reduce the heat to simmer and cook for the remaining time using the stir button occasionally. Blend to the consistency you prefer. Pour in the cream, cover and stir for a second or two without boiling. Season to taste, if necessary.
4 Ladle or pour the piping hot soup into bowls, top with chopped chives and serve immediately with hot crusty bread on the side.

JUG-STYLE SOUP MAKER

Put all the prepared ingredients (step 1 above) and other ingredients, except the cream, into the metal jug. Secure the lid in place. Select the chunky function and leave to cook. Blend to the consistency you prefer. Stir in the cream and season to taste, if necessary. Serve the soup as in step 4 above.

Parsnip Soup with Walnuts and Goat's Cheese

You can use blue Stilton in place of the goat's cheese as a delicious alternative.

SERVES 4
2 shallots
2 medium parsnips
Small piece of fresh root ginger
100g (3½oz) firm goat's cheese
Small handful of walnut pieces
2 tbsp olive oil
700ml (1¼ pints) vegetable or chicken stock
4 tbsp chopped parsley
1 tsp walnut oil, optional
Freshly milled black pepper, to taste
Hot garlic bread, to serve

1   Finely chop the shallots. Chop the parsnips into small pieces and finely grate the ginger.
2   Cut the goat's cheese into small pieces and roughly chop the walnuts.
3   Put the oil into the glass jar. Set the timer to 30 minutes and the temperature to high. Add the shallots, cover and cook for 1–2 minutes using the stir button occasionally. Add the parsnips, cover and cook for 3–4 minutes until steaming using the stir button occasionally.

4 Add the remaining ingredients except the goat's cheese, walnuts and walnut oil. Cover, stir to mix and bring to the boil for 2–3 minutes, then reduce the heat to simmer and cook for the remaining time, using the stir button occasionally. Blend to the consistency you prefer. Add the goat's cheese, walnuts and walnut oil (if using), cover and stir for a second or two. Season to taste, if necessary.

5 Ladle or pour the piping hot soup into bowls. Serve immediately with hot garlic bread.

JUG-STYLE SOUP MAKER

Put all the prepared ingredients (step 1 above) and other ingredients, except the goat's cheese, walnuts and walnut oil, into the metal jug. Secure the lid in place. Select the chunky function and leave to cook. Blend to the consistency you prefer, stir in the goat's cheese, walnuts and walnut oil (if using), and season to taste, if necessary. Serve the soup as in step 5 above.

Smoky Turnip, Parsnip and Carrot Soup

This unusual twist on classic ingredients has a distinctive, smoky, peppery taste.

SERVES 4
1 onion
6 small pink turnips
2 parsnips
4 carrots
2 tbsp olive oil
1 tsp smoked paprika pepper
2 tbsp lemon juice
700ml (1¼ pints) chicken or vegetable stock
Freshly milled black pepper, to taste
Sourdough croûtons, to serve

1   Finely chop the onion. Roughly chop the turnips, parsnips and carrots into small pieces.
2   Put the oil into the glass jar. Set the timer to 30 minutes and the temperature to high. Add the onion, cover and cook for 2 minutes, using the stir button occasionally, until it begins to steam, but has not browned too much. Add the turnips, parsnips and carrots, cover, stir and cook for 5 minutes, using the stir button occasionally, until they begin to steam.
3   Add the remaining ingredients, cover, stir to mix and bring to the boil for 2–3 minutes. Reduce the heat to simmer and cook for the remaining time using the stir button occasionally. Blend to the consistency you prefer. Season to taste, if necessary.
4   Ladle or pour the piping hot soup into bowls. Scatter a few sourdough croûtons on top and serve immediately.

JUG-STYLE SOUP MAKER
Put all the prepared ingredients (step 1 above) and other ingredients into the metal jug. Secure the lid in place. Select the purée function and leave to cook. Season to taste, if necessary. Serve the soup as in step 4 above.

Chunky Vegetable Broth

With this versatile soup, you can vary the vegetables to suit what's in your veg box.

SERVES 4
1 leek
2 garlic cloves
1 parsnip
2 carrots
2 kale leaves
2 tbsp olive oil
1 tbsp wholegrain mustard
200g can tomatoes in natural juice
700ml (1¼ pints) vegetable or chicken stock
Freshly milled black pepper, to taste
Grated Cheddar cheese and nutty brown bread rolls, to serve

1   Thinly slice the leek and crush the garlic. Roughly chop the parsnip and carrots into small pieces. Trim the tough stems from the frilly kale and roughly slice the leaves.
2   Put the oil into the glass jar. Set the timer to 30 minutes and the temperature to high. Add the leek, cover and cook for 3–4 minutes using the stir button occasionally until beginning to steam. Add the garlic, parsnip, carrots and kale. Cover, stir and cook for 4–5 minutes using the stir button occasionally until beginning to steam.
3   Add the remaining ingredients, cover, stir to mix and bring to the boil for 3 minutes. Reduce the heat to simmer and cook for the remaining time using the stir button occasionally. Blend, but leave the soup chunky. Season to taste, if necessary.
4   Ladle or pour the piping hot soup into bowls. Sprinkle over a little grated cheese and serve immediately with some nutty brown bread rolls.

JUG-STYLE SOUP MAKER
Put all the prepared ingredients (step 1 above) and other ingredients into the metal jug. Secure the lid in place. Select the chunky function and leave to cook. Season to taste, if necessary. Serve the soup as in step 4 above.

Minted Carrot and Leek Soup

Carrot and orange are a tried-and-tested match; add a little mint to take it to another level!

SERVES 4
1 leek
4 carrots
Small bunch of mint
2 tbsp olive oil
700ml (1¼ pints) chicken or vegetable stock
1 tsp grated orange zest
Freshly milled black pepper, to taste
Natural yogurt and a little oil, to serve

1   Thinly slice the leek. Roughly chop the carrots into small pieces. Pull the mint leaves from the stalks.
2   Put the oil into the glass jar. Set the timer to 30 minutes and the temperature to high. Add the sliced leek, cover and cook for 2–3 minutes, using the stir button occasionally, until steaming, but not browned too much. Add the carrots, cover, stir and cook for 3 minutes.
3   Add the remaining ingredients, cover, stir to mix and bring to the boil for 2 minutes. Reduce the heat to simmer and cook for the remaining time using the stir button occasionally. Blend to the consistency you prefer. Season to taste, if necessary.
4   Ladle or pour the piping hot soup into bowls. Spoon yogurt on top and drizzle over a few drops of oil. Serve immediately.

JUG-STYLE SOUP MAKER
Put all the prepared ingredients (step 1 above) and other ingredients into the metal jug. Secure the lid in place. Select the purée function and leave to cook. Season to taste, if necessary. Serve the soup as in step 4 above.

Garlic and Sweet Potato Soup

I often like to make this with meat stock, but use vegetable for a vegetarian dish. Don't be overwhelmed by the amount of garlic – it's strong but mellow.

SERVES 4
1 large onion
6 garlic cloves
550g (1lb 4oz) sweet potatoes
Small bunch of coriander
Small bunch of parsley
2 tbsp olive oil
1–2 drops of tabasco sauce
700ml (1¼ pints) meat, vegetable or chicken stock
Freshly milled black pepper, to taste
Slices of hot olive bread, to serve

1   Finely chop the onion and crush the garlic. Cut the sweet potatoes into small pieces. Pull the coriander leaves from the stalks. Finely chop the parsley.
2   Put the oil into the glass jar. Set the timer to 30 minutes and the temperature to high. Add the onion and garlic, cover and cook for 1–2 minutes, using the stir button occasionally. Add the sweet potato, cover and cook for 3–5 minutes until beginning to steam, using the stir button occasionally.
3   Add the remaining ingredients, cover, stir to mix and bring to the boil for 2–3 minutes. Reduce the heat to simmer and cook for the remaining time using the stir button occasionally. Blend to the consistency you prefer. Season to taste, if necessary.
4   Ladle or pour the piping hot soup into bowls. Serve immediately with hot olive bread.

JUG-STYLE SOUP MAKER
Put all the prepared ingredients (step 1 above) and other ingredients into the metal jug. Secure the lid in place. Select the chunky function and leave to cook. Blend to the consistency you prefer and season to taste, if necessary. Serve the soup as in step 4 above.

Celeriac and Rosemary Soup

Celeriac is a knobbly root vegetable tasting like a cross between celery and parsley.

SERVES 4
3 shallots
1 celeriac, about 500g (1lb 2oz)
1 green pepper
3 rosemary sprigs
2 tbsp olive oil
2 tbsp lemon juice
700ml (1¼ pints) vegetable or chicken stock
Freshly milled black pepper, to taste
Hot French bread, to serve

1 Finely chop the shallots. Peel the celeriac and cut into small pieces. Cut the pepper in half, remove the seeds and stalk and roughly chop. Pull the leaves from the rosemary sprigs.
2 Put the oil into the glass jar. Set the timer to 30 minutes and the temperature to high. Add the shallots, cover and cook for 2–3 minutes, using the stir button occasionally, until they begin to steam, but are not browned too much. Add the celeriac, cover, stir and cook for 5 minutes, using the stir button occasionally, until they begin to steam.
3 Add the remaining ingredients, cover, stir to mix and bring to the boil for 3–4 minutes. Reduce the heat to simmer and cook for the remaining time using the stir button occasionally. Blend to the consistency you prefer. Season to taste, if necessary.
4 Ladle or pour the piping hot soup into bowls. Serve immediately with hot French bread.

JUG-STYLE SOUP MAKER
Put all the prepared ingredients (step 1 above) and other ingredients into the metal jug. Secure the lid in place. Select the purée function and leave to cook. Season to taste, if necessary. Serve the soup as in step 4 above.

Fennel and Thyme Soup

A creamy anise and thyme taste makes this soup deliciously different. If you like, use thick natural yogurt in place of the cream.

SERVES 4
1 large onion
2–3 medium fennel bulbs, about 400g (14 oz)
2 celery sticks
4 sprigs of thyme
1 tbsp olive oil
2 tsp lemon juice
140ml (¼ pint) milk
600ml (1 pint) vegetable or chicken stock
Freshly milled white pepper, to taste
Single cream and croûtons, to serve

1   Finely chop the onion and fennel bulbs. Thinly slice the celery stalks. Pull the thyme leaves from the stalks.
2   Put the oil into the glass jar. Set the timer to 30 minutes and the temperature to high. Add the onion, cover and cook for 1 minute, using the stir button occasionally. Add the fennel and celery, cover and cook for 6–8 minutes until steaming, using the stir button occasionally.
3   Add the remaining ingredients, cover, stir to mix and bring to the boil for 3–4 minutes. Reduce the heat to simmer and cook for the remaining time using the stir button occasionally. Blend until smooth. Season to taste, if necessary.
4   Ladle or pour the piping hot soup into bowls. Top with a swirl of cream and croûtons and serve immediately.

JUG-STYLE SOUP MAKER
Put all the prepared ingredients (step 1 above) and other ingredients into the metal jug. Secure the lid in place. Select the purée function and leave to cook. Season to taste, if necessary. Serve the soup as in step 4 above.

Carrot, Apple and Spinach Soup

This is a really colourful soup with a fresh and tasty blend of flavours.

SERVES 4
1 dessert apple
1 red onion
500g (1lb 2oz) carrots
1 tbsp olive oil
150ml (¼ pint) unsweetened orange juice
700ml (1¼ pints) chicken or vegetable stock
Two large handfuls of baby spinach leaves
½ tsp coriander seeds
Freshly milled black pepper, to taste
Natural yogurt and a little oil, to serve

1   Peel, core and roughly chop the apple. Slice the onion. Roughly chop the carrots into small pieces.
2   Put the oil into the glass jar. Set the timer to 30 minutes and the temperature to high. Add the onion, cover and cook for 2–3 minutes, using the stir button occasionally, until steaming, but not browned too much. Add the carrots, cover, stir and cook for 6 minutes.
3   Add the remaining ingredients, cover, stir to mix and bring to the boil for 2–3 minutes. Reduce the heat to simmer and cook for the remaining time using the stir button occasionally. Blend to the consistency you prefer. Season to taste, if necessary.
4   Ladle or pour the piping hot soup into bowls. Spoon yogurt on top and drizzle over a few drops of oil. Serve immediately.

JUG-STYLE SOUP MAKER
Put all the prepared ingredients (step 1 above) and other ingredients into the metal jug. Secure the lid in place. Select the purée function and leave to cook. Season to taste, if necessary. Serve the soup as in step 4 above.

Traditional Onion Soup

This is my take on a much-loved, traditional soup.

SERVES 4
700g (1lb 9oz) onions
2 garlic cloves
2 tbsp cornflour
2 tbsp sunflower oil
700 ml (1¼ pints) beef stock
1 tbsp Worcestershire sauce
1–2 drops of tabasco, hot pepper sauce
Freshly milled black pepper, to taste
Finely grated cheese, chopped parsley and hot crusty bread, to serve

1   Thinly slice the onions and crush the garlic. Put the cornflour into a small cup and stir in 2–3 tablespoons of cold water until blended.
2   Put the oil into the glass jar. Set the timer to 30 minutes and the temperature to high. Add the onion and garlic, cover and cook for 6–8 minutes using the stir button occasionally.
3   Add the remaining ingredients, cover, stir to mix and bring to the boil for 2–3 minutes. Reduce the heat to simmer and cook for the remaining time using the stir button occasionally. Season to taste, if necessary.
4   Ladle or pour the piping hot soup into bowls. Scatter a little grated cheese and chopped parsley on top and serve immediately with hot crusty bread.

JUG-STYLE SOUP MAKER
Put all the prepared ingredients (step 1 above) and other ingredients into the metal jug. Secure the lid in place. Select the chunky function and leave to cook. Season to taste, if necessary. Serve the soup as in step 3 above.

Carrot and Beetroot Soup

Make sure the beetroots you buy aren't packed in vinegar, as this will spoil the flavour of the soup.

SERVES 4
1 onion
4 carrots
4 medium-sized cooked beetroots
2 tbsp olive oil
700ml (1¼ pints) vegetable or chicken stock
1 tsp fennel seeds
2 tsp wholegrain mustard
Freshly milled black pepper, to taste
Lemon wedges, to serve

1   Finely chop the onion. Roughly chop the carrots and beetroots into small pieces.
2   Put the oil into the glass jar. Set the timer to 30 minutes and the temperature to high. Add the onion, cover and cook for 1–2 minutes until starting to soften. Use the stir button occasionally.
3   Add the remaining ingredients, cover, stir to mix and bring to the boil for 4–6 minutes. Reduce the heat to simmer and cook for the remaining time using the stir button occasionally. Blend to the consistency you prefer. Season to taste, if necessary.
4   Ladle or pour the piping hot soup into bowls and serve immediately with lemon wedges to squeeze over.

JUG-STYLE SOUP MAKER
Put all the prepared ingredients (step 1 above) and other ingredients into the metal jug. Secure the lid in place. Select the purée function and leave to cook. Add the yogurt, replace the lid and blend for a second. Season to taste, if necessary. Serve the soup as in step 3 above.

Roasted Vegetable
and Chick Pea Soup

**Always keep some packets of frozen roasted mixed vegetables
in the freezer to make this speedy soup that is full of flavour.**

SERVES 4
Small bunch of parsley
500g packet frozen roasted vegetables
700ml (1¼ pints) chicken or vegetable stock
400g can chickpeas
2 tbsp tomato purée
Freshly milled black pepper, to taste
Hot granary rolls, to serve

1   Roughly chop the parsley. If the roasted vegetables are too large
    cut into smaller pieces.
2   Set the timer to 30 minutes and the temperature to high. Add all
    the ingredients, cover, stir, and bring to the boil for 4–5 minutes.
    Reduce the heat to simmer and cook for the remaining time
    using the stir button occasionally. Leave chunky or blend as you
    prefer. Season to taste, if necessary.
3   Ladle or spoon the piping hot soup into bowls and serve
    immediately with hot granary rolls.

JUG-STYLE SOUP MAKER
Thaw the vegetables if frozen and, if too large, cut into smaller
pieces. Put all the prepared ingredients (step 1 above) and other
ingredients into the metal jug. Secure the lid in place. Select the
chunky function and leave to cook. Leave chunky or blend as you
prefer. Season to taste, if necessary. Serve the soup as in step 3 above.

Stems and Stalks

This is where you can discover some exciting soup-making possibilities for the vegetables I've grouped together as stems and stalks. Broccoli and cauliflowers, with their florets, and slender vegetables like asparagus, celery and leeks, all are undoubted superfoods and an excellent source of vitamins – and should form a regular part of our diet. With your soup maker and these approachable flavoursome recipes, you can easily achieve that objective.

Broccoli and Walnut Soup

Use toasted hazelnuts or pine nuts in place of the walnuts if you prefer.

SERVES 4
1 onion
500g (1lb 2oz) broccoli florets
3 sprigs of thyme
1 tbsp sunflower oil
700ml (1¼ pints) chicken or vegetable stock
Large pinch of grated nutmeg
Handful of walnut pieces
Freshly milled black pepper, to taste
Rye bread, to serve

1 Finely chop the onion. If large, roughly cut the broccoli florets into smaller pieces. Pull the thyme leaves from the stalks.
2 Put the oil into the glass jar. Set the timer to 20 minutes and the temperature to high. Add the onion, cover and cook for 1–2 minutes until beginning to soften, using the stir button occasionally. Add the broccoli florets, cover and cook for 4–5 minutes until beginning to steam using the stir button occasionally.
3 Add the remaining ingredients except the walnut pieces, cover, stir to mix and bring to the boil for 3 minutes. Reduce the heat to simmer and cook for the remaining time using the stir button occasionally. Blend to the consistency you prefer. Add the walnut pieces, cover and blend for a second. Season to taste, if necessary.
4 Ladle or spoon the piping hot soup into bowls. Serve immediately with the rye bread.

JUG-STYLE SOUP MAKER
Put all the prepared ingredients (step 1 above) and other ingredients except the walnuts pieces into the metal jug. Secure the lid in place. Select the chunky function and leave to cook. Blend to the consistency you prefer. Stir in the walnut pieces and blend for a second. Season to taste, if necessary. Serve the soup as in step 4 above.

Leek and Potato Soup

A hearty soup that is the perfect choice on a chill autumn day.

SERVES 4
1 onion
1 garlic clove
1 medium potato
1 leek
1 celery stick
3 fresh sage leaves
2 tbsp sunflower oil
700ml (1¼ pints) chicken or vegetable stock
Freshly milled black pepper, to taste

1   Finely chop the onion and crush the garlic. Cut the potato into small pieces. Thinly slice the leek and celery.
2   Put the oil into the glass jar. Set the timer to 30 minutes and the temperature to high. Add the onion, cover and cook for 1–2 minutes until beginning to soften, using the stir button occasionally. Add the potato and leek, cover and cook for 4–5 minutes until beginning to steam, using the stir button occasionally.
3   Add the remaining ingredients, cover, stir to mix and bring to the boil for 5 minutes. Reduce the heat to simmer and cook for the remaining time using the stir button occasionally. Blend to the consistency you prefer. Season to taste, if necessary.
4   Ladle or spoon the piping hot soup into bowls. Serve immediately.

JUG-STYLE SOUP MAKER
Put all the prepared ingredients (step 1 above) and other ingredients into the metal jug. Secure the lid in place. Select the chunky function and leave to cook. Blend to the consistency you prefer. Season to taste, if necessary. Serve the soup as in step 4 above.

Asparagus and Pea Soup

The asparagus season is short, but when it is out of season you can use frozen asparagus instead.

SERVES 4
1 onion
400g (14oz) fresh asparagus
1 small lemon
4 sprigs of mint
1 tbsp sunflower oil
700ml (1¼ pints) chicken or vegetable stock
200g (7oz) petit pois peas
Freshly milled black pepper, to taste
Lemon wedges, to serve

1   Finely chop the onion. Trim the asparagus and cut into short pieces. Cut the lemon in half and squeeze out the juice. Pull the mint leaves from the stalks.
2   Put the oil into the glass jar. Set the timer to 20 minutes and the temperature to high. Add the onion, cover and cook for 1–2 minutes until beginning to soften, using the stir button occasionally.
3   Add the remaining ingredients, cover, stir to mix and bring to the boil for 1 minute. Reduce the heat to simmer and cook for the remaining time, using the stir button occasionally. Blend to the consistency you prefer. Season to taste, if necessary.
4   Ladle or spoon the piping hot soup into bowls. Serve immediately with lemon wedges to squeeze over.

JUG-STYLE SOUP MAKER
Put all the prepared ingredients (step 1 above) and other ingredients into the metal jug. Secure the lid in place. Select the chunky function and leave to cook. Blend to the consistency you prefer. Season to taste, if necessary. Serve the soup as in step 4 above.

Curried Cauliflower Soup

Cauliflower has a delicious creamy texture when puréed.

SERVES 4
1 onion
1 small leek
450g (1lb) cauliflower florets
1 tbsp sunflower oil
600ml (1 pint) chicken or vegetable stock
300ml (½ pint) milk
2–3 tsp curry paste
½ tsp turmeric
Freshly milled black pepper, to taste

1   Finely chop the onion and the leek. If large, roughly cut the cauliflower florets into smaller pieces.
2   Put the oil into the glass jar. Set the timer to 30 minutes and the temperature to high. Add the onion and leek, cover and cook for 2–3 minutes until beginning to soften, using the stir button occasionally. Add the broccoli florets, cover and cook for 4–5 minutes until beginning to steam, using the stir button occasionally.
3   Add the remaining ingredients, cover, stir to mix and bring to the boil for 4 minutes. Reduce the heat to simmer and cook for the remaining time, using the stir button occasionally. Blend to the consistency you prefer. Season to taste, if necessary.
4   Ladle or spoon the piping hot soup into bowls. Serve immediately.

JUG-STYLE SOUP MAKER
Put all the prepared ingredients (step 1 above) and other ingredients into the metal jug. Secure the lid in place. Select the chunky function and leave to cook. Blend to the consistency you prefer. Season to taste, if necessary. Serve the soup as in step 4 above.

Leek and Porcini Mushroom Soup

Dried mushrooms give an extra depth of flavour.

SERVES 4

4 dried porcini mushrooms

700ml (1¼ pints) chicken, mushroom or vegetable stock

2 shallots

280g (10oz) chestnut mushrooms

1 leek

2 sprigs of thyme

2 tbsp olive oil

Freshly milled black pepper, to taste

Truffle oil, to serve

1   Re-hydrate the porcini mushrooms. In a saucepan bring 300ml (½ pint) of the stock just to the boil. Place the porcini in a bowl and pour over the stock. Leave to stand for 30 minutes. Lift the mushrooms from the soaking liquid, check they are clean and thinly slice. Strain the soaking liquid through a fine meshed sieve or a piece of muslin and add it to the remaining stock.

2   Finely chop the shallots. Roughly chop the chestnut mushrooms. Thinly slice the leek. Pull the thyme leaves from the stalks.

3   Put the oil into the glass jar. Set the timer to 30 minutes and the temperature to high. Add the shallots, cover and cook for 1–2 minutes until beginning to soften, using the stir button occasionally. Add the leeks, cover and cook for 4–5 minutes until beginning to steam, using the stir button occasionally.

4 Add the remaining ingredients, cover, stir to mix and bring to the boil for 3 minutes. Reduce the heat to simmer and cook for the remaining time, using the stir button occasionally. Blend to the consistency you prefer. Season to taste, if necessary.
5 Ladle or spoon the piping hot soup into bowls. Drizzle over a few drops of the truffle oil and serve immediately.

JUG-STYLE SOUP MAKER

Put all the prepared ingredients (steps 1 and 2 above) and other ingredients into the metal jug. Secure the lid in place. Select the chunky function and leave to cook. Blend to the consistency you prefer. Season to taste, if necessary. Serve the soup as in step 5 above.

Vegetable and Pasta Soup

You can ring the changes with this soup by replacing the pasta shapes with rice or egg noodles.

SERVES 4
1 onion
1 celery stick
1 carrot
350g (12oz) broccoli florets
3 tomatoes
2 large handfuls of small spinach leaves
2 tbsp olive oil
700ml (1¼ pints) vegetable or chicken stock
1 tbsp wholegrain mustard
¼ tsp dried mixed herbs
Freshly milled black pepper, to taste
140g (5oz) small fresh pasta shapes

1   Finely chop the onion. Thinly slice the celery stick. Finely chop the carrot. If large, cut the broccoli into smaller pieces. Quarter the tomatoes. Shred the spinach leaves.
2   Put the oil into the glass jar. Set the timer to 25 minutes and the temperature to high. Add the onion, cover and cook for 1–2 minutes, using the stir button occasionally until it begins to steam, but without browning too much. Add the carrot and cauliflower florets, cover and cook for 4–5 minutes until beginning to steam, using the stir button occasionally.
3   Add the remaining ingredients except the pasta, cover, stir to mix and bring to the boil. Reduce the heat to simmer and cook for the remaining time, using the stir button occasionally.

4 While the soup is cooking, cook the pasta following the packet instructions. Leave the soup chunky or blend to the consistency you prefer. Season to taste, if necessary.

5 Spoon the hot pasta into bowls. Ladle or pour the piping hot soup over the pasta. Serve immediately.

JUG-STYLE SOUP MAKER

Put all the prepared ingredients (step 1 above) and other ingredients except the pasta into the metal jug. Secure the lid in place. Select the chunky function and leave to cook. Meanwhile cook the pasta, see step 4 above. Blend the soup to the consistency you prefer. Season the soup, if necessary, and serve as in step 5 above.

Broccoli, Courgette and Olive Soup

Cauliflower would work well as a substitute for the broccoli in this soup.

SERVES 4
1 onion
2 courgettes
350g (12oz) broccoli florets
Small handful of spinach leaves
125g (4½oz) pitted black olives
2 tbsp olive oil
700ml (1¼ pints) chicken or vegetable stock
1 tbsp lemon juice
Freshly milled black pepper, to taste
Toasted bruschetta, to serve

1   Finely chop the onion. Thinly slice the courgettes. If large, roughly cut the broccoli florets into smaller pieces. Thinly shred the spinach leaves. Slice the black olives.
2   Put the oil into the glass jar. Set the timer to 25 minutes and the temperature to high. Add the onion, cover and cook for 1–2 minutes until beginning to soften, using the stir button occasionally. Add the courgettes and broccoli florets, cover and cook for 4–5 minutes until beginning to steam, using the stir button occasionally.
3   Add the remaining ingredients, except the black olives, cover, stir to mix and bring to the boil for 3 minutes. Reduce the heat to simmer and cook for the remaining time, using the stir button occasionally. Blend to the consistency you prefer. Stir in the black olives and season to taste, if necessary.
4   Ladle or spoon the piping hot soup into bowls. Serve immediately with the toasted bruschetta.

JUG-STYLE SOUP MAKER
Put all the prepared ingredients except the black olives (step 1 above) and other ingredients into the metal jug. Secure the lid in place. Select the chunky function and leave to cook. Blend to the consistency you prefer. Stir in the black olives and season to taste, if necessary. Serve the soup as in step 4 above.

Tomato and Leek Soup

If you like a bit of heat, add a little curry paste to this smooth and warming soup.

SERVES 4
1 onion
2 garlic cloves
2 leeks, about 350g (12oz)
3 sun-dried tomatoes
1 tbsp sunflower oil
600ml (1 pint) chicken or vegetable stock
400g can tomatoes
Freshly milled black pepper, to taste
Garlic bread, to serve

1   Finely chop the onion and garlic. Thinly slice the leeks. Finely chop the sun-dried tomatoes.
2   Put the oil into the glass jar. Set the timer to 25 minutes and the temperature to high. Add the onion and garlic, cover and cook for 1–2 minutes until beginning to soften, using the stir button occasionally. Add the leeks, cover and cook for 4–5 minutes until beginning to steam, using the stir button occasionally.
3   Add the remaining ingredients, cover, stir to mix and bring to the boil for 2 minutes. Reduce the heat to simmer and cook for the remaining time, using the stir button occasionally. Blend to the consistency you prefer. Season to taste, if necessary.
4   Ladle or spoon the piping hot soup into bowls. Serve immediately with the garlic bread.

JUG-STYLE SOUP MAKER
Put all the prepared ingredients (step 1 above) and other ingredients into the metal jug. Secure the lid in place. Select the chunky function and leave to cook. Blend to the consistency you prefer. Season to taste, if necessary. Serve the soup as in step 4 above.

Celery and Herb Soup

Choose young celery roots and the stalks won't be too stringy.

SERVES 4
1 onion
2 celery roots
4 sprigs of mint
Small bunch of marjoram
Small bunch of basil
Small bunch of parsley
1 tbsp sunflower oil
700ml (1¼ pints) chicken or vegetable stock
Freshly milled black pepper, to taste

1 Finely chop the onion. Pull the celery roots apart, clean the sticks thoroughly and thinly slice. Pull all the herb leaves from the stalks.
2 Put the oil into the glass jar. Set the timer to 30 minutes and the temperature to high. Add the onion, cover and cook for 1–2 minutes until beginning to soften, using the stir button occasionally. Add the celery, cover and cook for 4–5 minutes until beginning to steam, using the stir button occasionally.
3 Add the remaining ingredients, cover, stir to mix and bring to the boil for 4 minutes. Reduce the heat to simmer and cook for the remaining time, using the stir button occasionally. Blend to the consistency you prefer. Season to taste, if necessary.
4 Ladle or spoon the piping hot soup into bowls. Serve immediately.

JUG-STYLE SOUP MAKER
Put all the prepared ingredients (step 1 above) and other ingredients into the metal jug. Secure the lid in place. Select the chunky function and leave to cook. Blend to the consistency you prefer. Season to taste, if necessary. Serve the soup as in step 4 above.

Celery and Red Lentil Soup

Red lentils don't need to be soaked before you use them. They thicken and add flavour to this soup.

SERVES 4
1 red onion
1 garlic clove
1 celery root
1 red chilli
4 sprigs of thyme
2 tbsp olive oil
850ml (1½ pints) chicken, mushroom or vegetable stock
150g (5½oz) red lentils
Freshly milled black pepper, to taste

1   Finely chop the onion and garlic. Pull the celery root apart, clean the sticks thoroughly and thinly slice. Cut the chilli in half, remove the stalk and seeds and finely chop. Pull the thyme leaves from the stalks.
2   Put the oil into the glass jar. Set the timer to 30 minutes and the temperature to high. Add the onion and garlic, cover and cook for 1–2 minutes until beginning to soften, using the stir button occasionally. Add the celery, cover and cook for 5 minutes until beginning to steam, using the stir button occasionally.
3   Add the remaining ingredients, cover, stir to mix and bring to the boil for 5 minutes. Reduce the heat to simmer and cook for the remaining time, using the stir button occasionally. Blend to the consistency you prefer. Season to taste, if necessary.
4   Ladle or spoon the piping hot soup into bowls. Serve immediately.

JUG-STYLE SOUP MAKER
Put all the prepared ingredients (step 1 above) and other ingredients into the metal jug. Secure the lid in place. Select the chunky function and leave to cook. Blend to the consistency you prefer. Season to taste, if necessary. Serve the soup as in step 4 above.

Cauliflower and Broccoli Soup with Cheese Toasts

Always a winning combination: cheese on toast plus soup!

SERVES 4

1 onion
250g (9oz) cauliflower florets
200g (7oz) broccoli florets
Large handful small spinach leaves
Small handful of parsley leaves
1 tbsp plain flour
1 tbsp olive oil
400ml (14fl oz) chicken or vegetable stock
300ml (½ pint) milk
Freshly milled black pepper, to taste

TOPPING
4–6 thick slices from a whole grain baguette
Soft garlic cream cheese, to spread

1   Finely chop the onion. If large, roughly cut the cauliflower and broccoli florets into smaller pieces. Roughly tear the spinach leaves. Chop the parsley. In a small bowl, mix the flour to a paste with a little cold water.

2   Put the oil into the glass jar. Set the timer to 30 minutes and the temperature to high. Add the onion, cover and cook for 1–2 minutes until beginning to soften, using the stir button occasionally. Add the cauliflower and broccoli florets, cover and cook for 4–5 minutes until beginning to steam, using the stir button occasionally.

3   Add the remaining ingredients, cover, stir to mix and bring to the boil for 4 minutes. Reduce the heat to simmer and cook for the remaining time, using the stir button occasionally. Blend to the consistency you prefer.

4 While the soup is cooking, make the cheese toasts. Toast the bread on both sides under a hot grill. Spread one side of the bread with the garlic cream cheese. Put back under the hot grill until golden. Cut each slice into four pieces. Season the soup to taste, if necessary.

5 Ladle or spoon the piping hot soup into bowls. Float the cheese toasts on top of the soup and serve immediately.

JUG-STYLE SOUP MAKER

Put all the prepared ingredients (step 1 above) and other ingredients into the metal jug. Secure the lid in place. Select the chunky function and leave to cook. Blend to the consistency you prefer. While the soup is cooking, make the cheese toasts (see step 4 above). Season the soup to taste, if necessary. Serve as in step 5 above.

Spring Onion, Asparagus and Halloumi Soup

Greek halloumi cheese was traditionally made with sheep's milk but now it is usually goat's milk. A firm cheese, it is delicious fried.

SERVES 4

6 spring onions
350g (12oz) asparagus
2 courgettes
Small bunch of fennel leaves
1 tbsp olive oil, plus extra
700ml (1¼ pints) chicken or vegetable stock
1 tbsp lemon juice
Freshly milled black pepper, to taste
4 slices halloumi cheese
Fennel leaves, to serve

1 Thinly slice the spring onions. Trim the asparagus and cut into short pieces. Cut the courgettes into small pieces. Pull the fennel leaves from the stalks and finely chop.

2 Put the tablespoon of oil into the glass jar. Set the timer to 20 minutes and the temperature to high. Add the spring onions, cover and cook for 1–2 minutes until beginning to soften, using the stir button occasionally. Add the courgettes, cover and cook for 4–5 minutes until beginning to steam, using the stir button occasionally.

3 Add the remaining ingredients except the halloumi cheese, cover, stir to mix and bring to the boil for 1 minute. Reduce the heat to simmer and cook for the remaining time using the stir button occasionally. Blend to the consistency you prefer. Season to taste, if necessary.

4 While the soup is cooking, heat a little extra oil in a frying pan. Cook the halloumi cheese on both sides until golden brown.
5 Put a slice of hot cheese into bowls. Ladle or pour the piping hot soup over the cheese. Top with fennel leaves and serve immediately.

JUG-STYLE SOUP MAKER
Put all the prepared ingredients (step 1 above) and other ingredients except the halloumi cheese into the metal jug. Secure the lid in place. Select the chunky function and leave to cook. Blend to the consistency you prefer. While the soup is cooking, heat the halloumi cheese (see step 4 above). Season the soup to taste, if necessary. Serve as in step 5 above.

Spiced Cauliflower and Beetroot Soup

These two simple ingredients are transformed by the spices in this recipe.

SERVES 4
1 large onion
350g (12oz) cauliflower florets
2 cooked beetroots, about 250g (9oz)
2 tbsp olive oil
1 tsp cumin seeds
1 tsp coriander seeds
1 tsp mustard seeds
700ml (1¼ pints) chicken or vegetable stock
2 tsp garam masala
Freshly milled black pepper, to taste
Hot herb naan bread, to serve

1 Finely chop the onion. If large, roughly cut the cauliflower florets into smaller pieces. Chop the beetroots into small pieces.
2 Put the oil into the glass jar. Set the timer to 25 minutes and the temperature to high. Add the onion and the cumin, coriander and mustard seeds, cover and cook for 1 minute until beginning to brown and soften but without letting the spices burn, using the stir button occasionally. Add the cauliflower florets, cover and cook for 4–5 minutes until beginning to steam, using the stir button occasionally.
3 Add the remaining ingredients, cover, stir to mix and bring to the boil for 3 minutes. Reduce the heat to simmer and cook for the remaining time, using the stir button occasionally. Blend to the consistency you prefer. Season to taste, if necessary.
4 Ladle or spoon the piping hot soup into bowls. Serve immediately with the hot herb naan bread.

JUG-STYLE SOUP MAKER
Put all the prepared ingredients (step 1 above) and other ingredients into the metal jug. Secure the lid in place. Select the chunky function and leave to cook. Blend to the consistency you prefer. Season to taste, if necessary. Serve the soup as in step 4 above.

Celery, Celeriac and Cauliflower Soup

This makes a great standby soup, particularly in autumn, when the ingredients are most plentiful.

SERVES 4
1 onion
2 celery sticks
250g (9oz) piece of celeriac
280g (10oz) cauliflower
1 tbsp olive oil
700ml (1¼ pints) chicken or vegetable stock
Freshly milled black pepper, to taste

1   Finely chop the onion. Thinly slice the celery. Peel the celeriac and cut into small pieces. If large, roughly cut the cauliflower into smaller pieces.
2   Put the oil into the glass jar. Set the timer to 25 minutes and the temperature to high. Add the onion, cover and cook for 1–2 minutes until beginning to soften, using the stir button occasionally. Add the celery, celeriac and cauliflower, cover and cook for 4–5 minutes until beginning to steam, using the stir button occasionally.
3   Add the remaining ingredients, cover, stir to mix and bring to the boil for 3 minutes. Reduce the heat to simmer and cook for the remaining time, using the stir button occasionally. Blend to the consistency you prefer. Season to taste, if necessary.
4   Ladle or spoon the piping hot soup into bowls. Serve immediately.

JUG-STYLE SOUP MAKER
Put all the prepared ingredients (step 1 above) and other ingredients into the metal jug. Secure the lid in place. Select the chunky function and leave to cook. Blend to the consistency you prefer. Season to taste, if necessary. Serve the soup as in step 4 above.

Purple Sprouting Broccoli and Peanut Soup

You can use cavolo nero or spinach leaves instead of the chard in this soup, depending on what you have available.

SERVES 4
1 onion
2 celery sticks
350g (12oz) purple sprouting broccoli
Two large handfuls of small chard leaves
1 tbsp olive oil
700ml (1¼ pints) chicken or vegetable stock
125g (4½oz) unsalted roasted peanuts
Freshly milled black pepper, to taste
Fresh sourdough breadcrumbs and olive oil, to serve

1 Finely chop the onion. Thinly slice the celery sticks. Cut the broccoli into small pieces. If large, roughly slice the chard leaves.
2 Put the oil into the glass jar. Set the timer to 20 minutes and the temperature to high. Add the onion, cover and cook for 1–2 minutes until beginning to soften, using the stir button occasionally. Add the celery, cover and cook for 4–5 minutes until beginning to steam, using the stir button occasionally.
3 Add the remaining ingredients, cover, stir to mix and bring to the boil for 3 minutes. Reduce the heat to simmer and cook for the remaining time using the stir button occasionally. Blend to the consistency you prefer. Season to taste, if necessary.
4 Ladle or spoon the piping hot soup into bowls. Sprinkle breadcrumbs over the soup and drizzle over a few drops of oil. Serve immediately.

JUG-STYLE SOUP MAKER
Put all the prepared ingredients (step 1 above) and other ingredients into the metal jug. Secure the lid in place. Select the chunky function and leave to cook. Blend to the consistency you prefer. Season to taste, if necessary. Serve the soup as in step 4 above.

Leaves

There are edible leaves in nearly every shade of green, from the pale hues of sea greens to the nearly-black colouring of cavolo nero – and there's red cabbage too. These are superfoods in abundance. The well-publicised health-giving properties of spinach, kale and all the other leaves which jostle here for attention are matched by their adaptability, which can be thoroughly explored through this appetising and tantalising selection of leaf-based soups.

Curly Kale, Corn and Pepper Soup

Kale comes in many varieties. The leaves are long and robust; to prepare them, cut away the stiff rib and use the frilly leaves.

SERVES 4
1 red onion
1 red pepper
6 large curly kale leaves
2 tbsp sunflower oil
850ml (1½ pints) chicken, mushroom or vegetable stock
200g (7oz) sweetcorn, fresh or frozen
1 tbsp chopped parsley
Freshly milled black pepper, to taste
Hot crusty bread, to serve

1 Roughly chop the onion. Cut the pepper in half, remove the stalk and seeds and slice. Cut and discard the stiff ribs from the curly kale leaves and thinly slice.
2 Put the oil into the glass jar. Set the timer to 30 minutes and the temperature to high. Add the onion, cover and cook for 2–3 minutes, using the stir button occasionally until beginning to brown. Add the curly kale leaves and sweetcorn, cover and cook for 4–5 minutes, using the stir button occasionally until beginning to steam.
3 Add the remaining ingredients, cover, stir to mix and bring to the boil for 5 minutes. Reduce the heat to simmer and cook for the remaining time, using the stir button occasionally until the vegetables are tender. Blend, but leave the soup chunky. Season to taste, if necessary.
4 Ladle or pour the piping hot soup into bowls and serve immediately with the hot crusty bread.

JUG-STYLE SOUP MAKER
Thaw the sweetcorn if frozen then put all the prepared ingredients (step 1 above) and other ingredients into the metal jug. Secure the lid in place. Select the chunky function and leave to cook. Season to taste, if necessary. Serve the soup as in step 4 above.

Watercress Soup with Lemongrass

Lemongrass has a more complex flavour than lemons, but if you don't have any you can use the rind and juice of half a lemon instead.

SERVES 4
6 spring onions
2 green peppers
2 lemongrass stalks
2 bunches of watercress
Small bunch of chives
2 tbsp olive oil
700ml (1¼ pints) vegetable or chicken stock
4 tbsp unsweetened orange juice
Freshly milled black pepper, to taste
3 tbsp crème fraîche or natural yogurt

1   Thinly slice the spring onions. Cut the peppers in half, remove the stalks and seeds and thinly slice. Pull the tough outer leaves off the lemongrass stalks and finely chop the remainder. Pull the watercress leaves from the stalks. Snip the chives with scissors.
2   Put the oil into the glass jar. Set the timer to 20 minutes and the temperature to high. Add the spring onions, cover and cook for 1 minute, using the stir button occasionally.
3   Add the remaining ingredients except the crème fraîche or natural yogurt. Cover, stir to mix and bring to the boil for 2–3 minutes, then reduce the heat to simmer and cook for the remaining time, using the stir button occasionally. Blend to the consistency you prefer. Add the crème fraîche or natural yogurt, cover and blend for a second. Season to taste, if necessary.
4   Ladle or pour the piping hot soup into bowls. Serve immediately.

JUG-STYLE SOUP MAKER
Put all the prepared ingredients (step 1 above) and other ingredients except the crème fraîche or natural yogurt into the metal jug. Secure the lid in place. Select the purée function and leave to cook. Add the crème fraîche or natural yogurt, replace the lid and blend for a second. Season to taste, if necessary. Serve the soup as in step 4 above.

Sea Greens and Fennel Soup

Sea greens or vegetables can be found on the fish counter in supermarkets and in some fishmongers. The selection changes with the seasons, so there is always something different to try.

SERVES 4

2 fennel bulbs
2 courgettes
2 pak choi
6 spring onions
1 small lemon
2.5cm (1in) piece of root ginger
3 large handfuls of sea vegetables
2 large handfuls of samphire
Small bunch of fennel leaves
2 tbsp olive oil
425ml (¾ pint) chicken or vegetable stock
425ml (¾ pint) fish or vegetable stock
Freshly milled black pepper, to taste

1   Finely chop the fennel bulbs. Cut the courgettes into small pieces. Thinly slice the pak choi and the spring onions. Grate the rind from the lemon, cut in half and squeeze out the juice. Finely grate the root ginger. Cut the sea vegetables into small pieces. Break the tender shoots of samphire off the thick stringy stalks. Finely chop the fennel leaves, saving a little to garnish the soup.
2   Put the oil into the glass jar. Set the timer to 25 minutes and the temperature to high. Add the chopped fennel bulbs, cover and cook for 3 minutes using the stir button occasionally until beginning to soften, but without browning too much. Add the courgettes, pak choi and spring onions, cover and cook for 2–3 minutes, using the stir button occasionally, until beginning to steam.

3   Add the remaining ingredients except the sea vegetables, samphire and the reserved chopped fennel leaves. Cover, stir to mix and bring to the boil for 2–3 minutes, then reduce the heat to simmer and cook for the remaining time, using the stir button occasionally. Four minutes before the end of the cooking time, add the sea vegetables and the samphire. Blend to the consistency you prefer. Season to taste, if necessary.
4   Ladle or pour the piping hot soup into bowls. Sprinkle over the reserved chopped fennel leaves and serve immediately.

JUG-STYLE SOUP MAKER
Put all the prepared ingredients, except the fennel leaf garnish (step 1 above), and all the other ingredients, except for the sea vegetables and the samphire, into the metal jug. Secure the lid in place. Select the purée function and leave to cook. Four minutes before the end of the cooking time, add the sea vegetables and the samphire. Season to taste, if necessary. Serve the soup as in step 4 above.

Spinach and Miso Soup with Noodles

You'll find miso paste in health food shops and the World Foods sections of supermarkets. Miso is sold in sachets or jars, either as a paste or as granules.

SERVES 4
6 spring onions
350g (12oz) spinach leaves
1 tbsp olive oil
700ml (1¼ pints) chicken or vegetable stock
3 x 8g sachets miso paste
Freshly milled black pepper, to taste
300g packet of ready-cooked fine-thread egg noodles
Sesame oil or olive oil, to serve

1   Thinly slice the spring onions. Roughly chop the spinach leaves.
2   Put the oil into the glass jar. Set the timer to 15 minutes and the temperature to high. Add the spring onions, cover and cook for 1 minute, using the stir button occasionally. Add the spinach, cover and cook for 3 minutes until steaming, using the stir button occasionally.
3   Add the remaining ingredients except the noodles. Cover, stir to mix and bring to the boil, then reduce the heat to simmer and cook for 10 minutes, using the stir button occasionally. Add the noodles and cook for the remaining time. Season to taste, if necessary.
4   Ladle or pour the piping hot soup into bowls. Drizzle with a drop or two of sesame oil or olive oil. Serve immediately.

JUG-STYLE SOUP MAKER
Put all the prepared ingredients (step 1 above) and other ingredients except the noodles into the metal jug. Secure the lid in place. Select the chunky function and leave to cook. While the soup is cooking, cook the noodles according to the packet instructions. Season to taste, if necessary. Heap the piping hot noodles into bowls and ladle or pour the piping hot soup over. Serve the soup as in step 4 above.

SUPERFOOD SOUPS

Greens and Pea Soup

Using different mixes of greens will give endless variations to this soup.

SERVES 4
1 onion
2 garlic cloves
350g (12oz) mixed greens such as Swiss chard,
   cavolo nero, kale or spinach
Small bunch of parsley
2 tbsp olive oil
700ml (1¼ pints) vegetable or chicken stock
140g (5oz) peas, fresh or frozen
Freshly milled black pepper, to taste
Toasted pine nuts and hot crusty bread, to serve

1   Roughly chop the onion and garlic. Thinly slice the mixed greens, discarding any tough stalks. Pull the parsley sprigs from the stalks and finely chop.
2   Put the oil into the glass jar. Set the timer to 25 minutes and the temperature to high. Add the onion and garlic, cover and cook for 1–2 minutes, using the stir button occasionally until beginning to brown. Add the mixed greens, cover and cook for 5–6 minutes, using the stir button occasionally until beginning to steam.
3   Add the remaining ingredients, cover, stir to mix and bring to the boil for 4 minutes. Reduce the heat to simmer and cook for the remaining time, using the stir button occasionally until the vegetables are tender. Blend, but leave the soup chunky and season to taste, if necessary.
4   Ladle or pour the piping hot soup into bowls. Sprinkle over some toasted pine nuts and serve immediately with hot crusty bread.

JUG-STYLE SOUP MAKER
Thaw the peas if you are using frozen, then put all the prepared ingredients (step 1 above) and other ingredients into the metal jug. Secure the lid in place. Select the chunky function and leave to cook. Season to taste, if necessary. Serve the soup as in step 4 above.

Spiced Red Cabbage and Apple Soup

Always a favourite soup with its sweet and sour taste.

SERVES 4
1 red onion
350g (12oz) red cabbage
1 small orange
1 eating apple
2 tbsp olive oil
700ml (1¼ pints) vegetable or chicken stock
1 tbsp red wine vinegar
1 tbsp clear honey
Freshly milled black pepper, to taste
Chopped parsley and hot crusty bread, to serve

1   Roughly chop the onion. Finely chop the red cabbage, discarding
    any tough stalks. Finely grate the rind from the orange, cut in
    half and squeeze out the juice. Core and chop the apple.
2   Put the oil into the glass jar. Set the timer to 30 minutes and the
    temperature to high. Add the onion, cover and cook for
    2–3 minutes, using the stir button occasionally until beginning
    to brown. Add the red cabbage and apple, cover and cook for
    5–6 minutes, using the stir button occasionally until beginning
    to steam.
3   Add the remaining ingredients, cover, stir to mix and bring to
    the boil for 4 minutes. Reduce the heat to simmer and cook for
    the remaining time, using the stir button occasionally until the
    vegetables are tender. Blend, but leave the soup chunky. Season
    to taste, if necessary.
4   Ladle or pour the piping hot soup into bowls. Sprinkle over a little
    chopped parsley and serve immediately with hot crusty bread.

JUG-STYLE SOUP MAKER
Put all the prepared ingredients (step 1 above) and other ingredients
into the metal jug. Secure the lid in place. Select the chunky function
and leave to cook. Season to taste, if necessary. Serve the soup as in
step 4 above.

Savoy Cabbage and Carrot Soup

Savoy cabbage looks very attractive with its crimped edges.

SERVES 4
1 red onion
2 carrots
350g (12oz) savoy cabbage
2 tbsp olive oil
850ml (1½ pints) vegetable or chicken stock
2 tbsp wholegrain mustard
Freshly milled black pepper, to taste
Hot nutty rolls, to serve

1 Roughly chop the onion, slice the carrots and finely chop the savoy cabbage, discarding any tough stalks.
2 Put the oil into the glass jar. Set the timer to 30 minutes and the temperature to high. Add the onion, cover and cook for 2–3 minutes, using the stir button occasionally until beginning to brown. Add the savoy cabbage and carrots, cover and cook for 5–6 minutes, using the stir button occasionally, until beginning to steam.
3 Add the remaining ingredients, cover, stir to mix and bring to the boil for 4 minutes. Reduce the heat to simmer and cook for the remaining time, using the stir button occasionally, until the vegetables are tender. Blend, but leave the soup chunky. Season to taste, if necessary.
4 Ladle or pour the piping hot soup into bowls. Serve immediately with hot nutty rolls.

JUG-STYLE SOUP MAKER
Put all the prepared ingredients (step 1 above) and other ingredients into the metal jug. Secure the lid in place. Select the chunky function and leave to cook. Season to taste, if necessary. Serve the soup as in step 4 above.

Kale Soup with Feta Cheese

Feta has a tangy, slightly salty taste and crumbles easily. For a different texture and flavour – mellow and melting – try torn pieces of mozzarella instead.

SERVES 4
1 onion
2 celery sticks
4 large handfuls of small kale leaves
Small bunch of parsley
175g (6oz) feta cheese
2 tbsp olive oil
850ml (1½ pints) chicken, mushroom or vegetable stock
Freshly milled black pepper, to taste
French bread, to serve

1   Roughly chop the onion. Slice the celery sticks. Cut and discard the stiff ribs of the kale and roughly slice. Pull the parsley sprigs from the stalks. Crumble the feta cheese.
2   Put the oil into the glass jar. Set the timer to 30 minutes and the temperature to high. Add the onion, cover and cook for 2–3 minutes, using the stir button occasionally until beginning to brown. Add the kale leaves and celery, cover and cook for 5–6 minutes, using the stir button occasionally until beginning to steam.
3   Add the remaining ingredients except the feta cheese. Cover, stir to mix and bring to the boil for 5 minutes. Reduce the heat to simmer and cook for the remaining time, using the stir button occasionally until the vegetables are tender. Blend, but leave the soup chunky. Tip the crumbled cheese into the soup. Replace the lid, stir to mix. Season to taste, if necessary.
4   Ladle or pour the piping hot soup into bowls. Serve immediately with French bread.

JUG-STYLE SOUP MAKER
Put all the prepared ingredients except the feta cheese (step 1 above) and other ingredients into the metal jug. Secure the lid in place. Select the chunky function and leave to cook. Stir the feta cheese into the soup. Season to taste, if necessary. Serve the soup as in step 4 above.

Sorrel and Salad Leaf Soup

Sorrel leaves have a sharp, fresh, lemon flavour.

SERVES 4
6 spring onions
4 large handfuls of large sorrel leaves
1 tbsp olive oil
4 large handfuls of small mixed salad leaves
700ml (1¼ pints) vegetable or chicken stock
Freshly milled black pepper, to taste
Rice crackers, to serve

1 Slice the spring onions. Cut and discard any tough stems on the
   sorrel leaves and roughly chop.
2 Put the oil into the glass jar. Set the timer to 20 minutes and the
   temperature to high. Add the spring onions, cover and cook for 1
   minute, using the stir button occasionally. Add the sorrel leaves,
   cover and cook for 1–2 minutes until steaming, using the stir
   button occasionally.
3 Add the remaining ingredients, cover, stir to mix and bring to
   the boil for 3–4 minutes. Reduce the heat to simmer and cook
   for the remaining time using the stir button occasionally. Blend
   until smooth. Season to taste, if necessary.
4 Ladle or pour the piping hot soup into bowls. Serve immediately
   with rice crackers.

JUG-STYLE SOUP MAKER
Put all the prepared ingredients (step 1 above) and other ingredients
into the metal jug. Secure the lid in place. Select the purée function
and leave to cook. Season to taste, if necessary. Serve the soup as in
step 4 above.

Herb and Pasta Soup

These may be ingredients you'd expect to see in a salad, but they are delicious when cooked.

SERVES 4
1 onion
1 garlic clove
1 small cos lettuce
1 small bunch of rocket
1 small bunch of parsley
1 bunch of chives
4 sprigs of oregano
100g (3½oz) fresh linguine pasta
2 tbsp olive oil
700ml (1¼ pints) chicken or vegetable stock
150ml (¼ pint) passata
Freshly milled black pepper, to taste
Grated Parmesan or pecorino cheese and chilli oil, to serve

1 Roughly chop the onion and garlic. Shred the cos lettuce. Roughly chop the rocket, parsley and chives discarding any tough stalks. Pull the oregano leaves from the stalks. Cut the linguine into short lengths.

2 Put the oil into the glass jar. Set the timer to 20 minutes and the temperature to high. Add the onion, cover and cook for 1–2 minutes, using the stir button occasionally, until beginning to soften. Add the lettuce, cover and cook for 3–4 minutes, using the stir button occasionally, until beginning to steam.

3 Add the remaining ingredients except the linguine. Cover, stir to mix and bring to the boil for 3 minutes. Reduce the heat to simmer and cook for the remaining time, using the stir button occasionally.

4   While the soup is cooking, cook the linguine following the packet instructions. Blend the soup to the consistency you prefer. Season to taste, if necessary.

5   Spoon the piping hot pasta into soup bowls. Ladle or pour the piping hot soup over the pasta. Serve immediately with a drizzle of chilli oil and a sprinkling of the grated cheese.

JUG-STYLE SOUP MAKER

Put all the prepared ingredients except the linguine (step 1 above) and other ingredients into the metal jug. Secure the lid in place. Select the chunky function and leave to cook. Blend to the consistency you prefer. Season to taste, if necessary. Meanwhile cook the linguine, see step 4 above. Stir the hot pasta into the soup. Serve the soup as in step 5 above.

Cavolo Nero and Mushroom Soup

I think 'Italy' when I make this soup. It's a holiday in a bowl!

SERVES 4
2 onions
2 garlic cloves
6 large cavolo nero leaves
200g (7oz) mushrooms
2 tbsp olive oil
700ml (1¼ pints) chicken, mushroom or vegetable stock
1 tsp crushed fennel seeds
1 tbsp lemon juice
Freshly milled black pepper, to taste
Brown sourdough bread, to serve

1   Finely chop the onions and slice the garlic. Cut and discard the ribs of the cavolo nero and roughly slice. Slice the mushrooms.
2   Put the oil into the glass jar. Set the timer to 30 minutes and the temperature to high. Add the onion and garlic, cover and cook for 3–4 minutes, using the stir button occasionally until beginning to soften and brown. Add the cavolo nero leaves and mushrooms, cover and cook for 5–6 minutes, using the stir button occasionally until beginning to steam.
3   Add the remaining ingredients, cover, stir to mix and bring to the boil for 5 minutes. Reduce the heat to simmer and cook for the remaining time, using the stir button occasionally until the vegetables are tender. Blend, but leave the soup chunky. Season to taste, if necessary.
4   Ladle or pour the piping hot soup into bowls. Serve immediately with brown sourdough bread.

JUG-STYLE SOUP MAKER
Put all the prepared ingredients (step 1 above) and other ingredients into the metal jug. Secure the lid in place. Select the chunky function and leave to cook. Season to taste, if necessary. Serve the soup as in step 4 above.

Spinach and Egg Soup

You garnish this green soup with bright flecks of chopped, hard-boiled egg, added at the end.

SERVES 4
2 onions
1 small lemon
250g (9oz) spinach leaves
3 eggs
2 tbsp sunflower oil
700ml (1¼ pints) vegetable or chicken stock
Freshly milled black pepper, to taste
150ml (¼ pint) natural yogurt

1   Finely chop the onions. Grate the rind from half the lemon, cut in half and squeeze out the juices. Roughly chop the spinach. Hard-boil the eggs, then peel and finely chop. Put the eggs to one side till later.
2   Put the oil into the glass jar. Set the timer to 20 minutes and the temperature to high. Add the onion, cover and cook for 1–2 minutes, using the stir button occasionally until beginning to soften.
3   Add the remaining ingredients except the chopped eggs and yogurt. Cover, stir to mix and bring to the boil for 2–3 minutes, then reduce the heat to simmer and cook for the remaining time, using the stir button occasionally. Blend to the consistency you prefer. Add the natural yogurt, cover and blend for a second. Season to taste, if necessary.
4   Ladle or pour the piping hot soup into bowls. Top each bowl with some chopped egg. Serve immediately.

JUG-STYLE SOUP MAKER
Put all the prepared ingredients except the eggs (step 1 above) and other ingredients except the natural yogurt into the metal jug. Secure the lid in place. Select the chunky function and leave to cook. Add the natural yogurt, replace the lid and blend for a second or two. Season to taste, if necessary. Serve the soup as in step 4 above.

Oriental Vegetable Soup

Look in farmers' markets and specialist stores for these leaves.

SERVES 4
2 spring onions
200g (7oz) Chinese leaves
1 pak choi
1 red chilli
1 lime
4 large handfuls of Asian vegetable leaves, such as
    choi sum, tatsoi or mizuna, or use small spinach leaves
2 tbsp olive oil
2 tbsp low-salt soy sauce
700ml (1¼ pints) vegetable or chicken stock
Freshly milled black pepper, to taste
Crushed toasted hazelnuts, to serve

1 Slice the spring onions. Shred the Chinese leaves and the pak
   choi. Cut the chilli in half, remove the seeds and stalk and thinly
   slice. Finely grate the lime, cut in half and squeeze the juice.
   Roughly chop the Asian vegetable leaves or the spinach leaves.
2 Put the oil into the glass jar. Set the timer to 20 minutes and the
   temperature to high. Add the spring onions, cover and cook for 1
   minute, using the stir button occasionally. Add the Chinese
   leaves and pak choi, cover and cook for 2–3 minutes until
   steaming, using the stir button occasionally.
3 Add the remaining ingredients, cover, stir to mix and bring to the
   boil for 3–4 minutes, then reduce the heat to simmer and cook for
   the remaining time using the stir button occasionally. Blend to
   the consistency of your choice. Season to taste, if necessary.
4 Ladle or pour the piping hot soup into bowls. Sprinkle over a
   few crushed hazelnuts and serve immediately.

JUG-STYLE SOUP MAKER
Put all the prepared ingredients (step 1 above) and other ingredients
into the metal jug. Secure the lid in place. Select the chunky function
and leave to cook. Season to taste, if necessary. Serve the soup as in
step 4 above.

Swiss Chard Soup with Couscous

**Use bulgur wheat in place of the couscous if you prefer –
it will give a chewy texture.**

SERVES 4
1 onion
250g (9oz) Swiss chard leaves
1 orange
3–4 sprigs of thyme
2 tbsp olive oil
850ml (1½ pints) chicken or vegetable stock
400g can tomatoes
100g (3½oz) large couscous
Freshly milled black pepper, to taste

1   Roughly chop the onion and roughly slice the Swiss chard
    leaves. Finely grate the rind from half the orange, cut in half and
    squeeze out the juice. Pull the thyme leaves from the stalks.
2   Put the oil into the glass jar. Set the timer to 25 minutes and the
    temperature to high. Add the onion, cover and cook for 1–2 minutes,
    using the stir button occasionally until beginning to brown. Add
    the Swiss chard leaves, cover and cook for 4–5 minutes, using the
    stir button occasionally, until beginning to steam.
3   Add the remaining ingredients except the couscous. Cover, stir to
    mix and bring to the boil for 4 minutes. Reduce the heat to simmer
    and cook for the remaining time, using the stir button occasionally.
4   While the soup is cooking, cook the couscous following the
    packet instructions. Blend the soup leaving it chunky. Stir the
    hot couscous into the soup. Season to taste, if necessary.
5   Ladle or pour the piping hot soup into bowls and serve immediately.

JUG-STYLE SOUP MAKER
Put all the prepared ingredients (step 1 above) and other ingredients
except the couscous into the metal jug. Secure the lid in place. Select
the chunky function and leave to cook. While the soup is cooking
follow step 4 above to cook the couscous. Season the soup to taste, if
necessary. Serve the soup as in step 5 above.

Leaves and Spiced Tomato Soup

This delicious soup has the taste of goulash, but no meat.

SERVES 4
2 onions
1 potato
250g (9oz) mixed greens such as Swiss chard, cavolo nero,
    kale or spinach
1 red pepper
2 tbsp olive oil
700ml (1¼ pints) vegetable or chicken stock
150ml (¼ pint) passata
1 tbsp paprika pepper
2 tsp caraway seeds
Freshly milled black pepper, to taste
Thick Greek yogurt, to serve

1   Roughly chop the onions, cut the potato into small dice and
    thinly slice the mixed greens, discarding any tough stalks. Cut
    the pepper in half, remove the seeds and stalk and thinly slice.
2   Put the oil into the glass jar. Set the timer to 30 minutes and the
    temperature to high. Add the onion, cover and cook for 1–2
    minutes, using the stir button occasionally until beginning to
    soften and brown. Add the potato and mixed greens, cover and
    cook for 5–6 minutes, using the stir button occasionally until
    beginning to steam.

3   Add the remaining ingredients, cover, stir to mix and bring to
    the boil for 4 minutes. Reduce the heat to simmer and cook for
    the remaining time, using the stir button occasionally until the
    vegetables are tender. Blend, but leave the soup chunky. Season
    to taste, if necessary.
4   Ladle or pour the piping hot soup into bowls. Add a spoonful of
    yogurt to each bowl and serve immediately.

JUG-STYLE SOUP MAKER
Put all the prepared ingredients (step 1 above) and other ingredients
into the metal jug. Secure the lid in place. Select the chunky function
and leave to cook. Season to taste, if necessary. Serve the soup as in
step 4 above.

Nettle and Dandelion Soup

You can find nettles growing in the garden or on open ground, but avoid places where they may have been sprayed with pesticides. Wear gloves to pick the new tiny leaves.

SERVES 4

6 large handfuls of young nettle tops or spinach leaves
6 large handfuls of small young dandelion leaves
    or spinach leaves
2 onions
1 baking potato, about 225g (8oz)
1 tbsp olive oil
850ml (1½ pints) vegetable or chicken stock
1 tbsp lemon juice
Freshly milled black pepper, to taste
Thick yogurt, to serve

1   Thoroughly wash the nettle tops and dandelion leaves or spinach leaves in plenty of cold water. Roughly chop the onions and cut the potato into small dice.
2   Put the oil into the glass jar. Set the timer to 25 minutes and the temperature to high. Add the onion, cover and cook for 1–2 minutes, using the stir button occasionally, until beginning to steam, but without browning too much. Add the potato, cover and cook for 4–5 minutes, using the stir button occasionally until beginning to steam.
3   Add the remaining ingredients, cover, stir to mix and bring to the boil for 3–4 minutes. Reduce the heat to simmer and cook for the remaining time using the stir button occasionally. Blend to the consistency you prefer. Season to taste, if necessary.
4   Ladle or pour the piping hot soup into bowls. Top each bowl with a blob of yogurt and serve immediately.

JUG-STYLE SOUP MAKER

Put all the prepared ingredients (step 1 above) and other ingredients into the metal jug. Secure the lid in place. Select the purée function and leave to cook. Season to taste, if necessary. Serve the soup immediately as in step 4 above.

Pods

Peas and beans are little bundles of energy, delivered in pods: nature's parcels. They are diminutive superfoods, so use them plentifully and often. There's lots of choice here: recipes for haricot beans, broad beans, pinto beans, flageolets and fashionable edamame; also for petit pois peas, sugar-snap peas and my version of the classic pea soup. These are convenient, any-time-of-the-year soups – always satisfying, always welcome.

Pea Soup

There are always peas available, fresh or usually lurking at the bottom of the freezer, making this an easy, standby soup.

SERVES 4
1 onion
Small bunch of mint
Small bunch of flat-leafed parsley
2 tsp olive oil
500g (1lb 2oz) peas, fresh or frozen
850ml (1½ pints) vegetable or chicken stock
150ml (¼ pint) natural yogurt
Freshly milled black pepper, to taste
Olive oil, to serve

1   Finely chop the onion. Keeping the mint and parsley separate, pull both the mint and parsley leaves from the stalks. Finely chop a few of the mint leaves and a few of the parsley leaves for garnishing the soup.
2   Put the oil into the glass jar. Set the timer to 25 minutes and the temperature to high. Add the onion, cover and cook for 2 minutes, using the stir button occasionally. Add the peas, cover and cook for 5–6 minutes until steaming, using the stir button occasionally.
3   Add the remaining ingredients except the yogurt. Cover, stir, and bring to the boil for 2–3 minutes, then reduce the heat to simmer and cook for the remaining time using the stir button occasionally. Blend until smooth. Add the yogurt, cover and stir for a few seconds without boiling. Season to taste, if necessary.
4   Ladle or pour the the piping hot soup into bowls. Serve with a little oil drizzled over the soup and a sprinkling of chopped mint and parsley leaves. Serve immediately.

JUG-STYLE SOUP MAKER
Thaw the peas if frozen. Put all the prepared ingredients except the reserved chopped mint and parsley leaves (step 1 above) and other ingredients except the yogurt into the metal jug. Secure the lid in place. Select the purée function and leave to cook. Stir in the yogurt. Season to taste, if necessary. Serve the soup as in step 4 above.

Edamame, Lime and Lemon Soup

Edamame beans are soya beans. These small bright green gems give a lovely flavour to soups.

SERVES 4
1 onion
1 carrot
1 lime
1 small lemon
Small handful of fennel leaves
1 tbsp olive oil
450g (1lb) edamame beans, fresh or frozen
700ml (1¼ pints) vegetable, mushroom or chicken stock
Freshly milled black pepper, to taste
Sourdough bread, to serve

1 Finely chop the onion and carrot. Grate the rind from half of the lime and the lemon. Cut each in half and squeeze out all the juices. Finely chop the fennel leaves.

2 Put the oil into the glass jar. Set the timer to 25 minutes and the temperature to high. Add the onion and carrot, cover and cook for 2 minutes, using the stir button occasionally. Add the edamame beans, cover and cook for 3–4 minutes, using the stir button occasionally, until beginning to steam.

3 Add the remaining ingredients, cover, stir to mix and bring to the boil for 3–4 minutes. Reduce the heat to simmer and cook for the remaining time, using the stir button occasionally. Blend to the consistency you prefer. Season to taste, if necessary.

4 Ladle or pour the piping hot soup into bowls and serve immediately with sourdough bread.

JUG-STYLE SOUP MAKER

Thaw the edamame beans if frozen. Put all the prepared ingredients (step 1 above) and other ingredients into the metal jug. Secure the lid in place. Select the chunky function and leave to cook. Blend to the consistency you prefer. Season to taste, if necessary. Serve the soup as in step 4 above.

Broad Bean Soup

**If you are picking or growing broad beans in their pods, double
the weight given in the ingredients list.**

SERVES 4
1 onion
1 garlic clove
2 carrots
1 tbsp olive oil
500g (1lb 2oz) broad beans, fresh or frozen
700ml (1¼ pints) vegetable or chicken stock
Freshly milled black pepper, to taste

1   Roughly chop the onion, crush the garlic and thinly slice the
    carrots.
2   Put the oil into the glass jar. Set the timer to 30 minutes and the
    temperature to high. Add the onion, cover and cook for 2
    minutes, using the stir button occasionally. Add the carrots,
    broad beans and garlic, cover and cook for 5–6 minutes until
    steaming, using the stir button occasionally.
3   Add the remaining ingredients, cover, stir to mix and bring to
    the boil for 3–4 minutes. Reduce the heat to simmer and cook
    for the remaining time using the stir button occasionally. Blend
    to the consistency you prefer. Season to taste, if necessary.
4   Ladle or pour the piping hot soup into bowls and serve immediately.

JUG-STYLE SOUP MAKER
Thaw the broad beans if frozen. Put all the prepared ingredients
(step 1 above) and other ingredients into the metal jug. Secure the lid
in place. Select the chunky function and leave to cook. Blend to the
consistency you prefer. Season to taste, if necessary. Serve the soup
as in step 4 above.

Peas, Corn and Fennel Soup

The vegetables in this recipe will naturally thicken the soup.

SERVES 4
1 red onion
1 fennel bulb
1 tbsp olive oil
850ml (1½ pints) vegetable, mushroom or chicken stock
350g (12oz) peas, fresh or frozen
150g (5½oz) sweetcorn, fresh or frozen
1 tsp fennel seeds
Freshly milled black pepper, to taste

1   Finely chop the onion and thinly slice the fennel bulb.
2   Put the oil into the glass jar. Set the timer to 30 minutes and the
    temperature to high. Add the onion, cover and cook for 1–2
    minutes using the stir button occasionally. Add the fennel bulb,
    cover and cook for 4–5 minutes until steaming, using the stir
    button occasionally.
3   Add the remaining ingredients, cover, stir to mix and bring to
    the boil for 3–4 minutes. Reduce the heat to simmer and cook
    for the remaining time using the stir button occasionally. Blend
    to the consistency you prefer. Season to taste, if necessary.
4   Ladle or pour the piping hot soup into bowls and serve immediately.

JUG-STYLE SOUP MAKER
Thaw the peas and sweetcorn if frozen. Put all the prepared
ingredients (step 1 above) and other ingredients into the metal jug.
Secure the lid in place. Select the chunky function and leave to cook.
Blend to the consistency you prefer. Season to taste, if necessary.
Serve the soup as in step 4 above.

Broad Bean and Mushroom Soup

For a change, use cooked flageolet or borlotti beans in place of the broad beans.

SERVES 4
1 onion
2 garlic cloves
200g (7oz) chestnut mushrooms
1 small lemon
2 tbsp olive oil
350g (12oz) broad beans, fresh or frozen
700ml (1¼ pints) vegetable, mushroom or chicken stock
Freshly milled black pepper, to taste

1 Roughly chop the onion and garlic. Slice the mushrooms. Finely grate the lemon, cut in half and squeeze out the juice.
2 Put the oil into the glass jar. Set the timer to 30 minutes and the temperature to high. Add the onion and garlic, cover and cook for 2 minutes using the stir button occasionally. Add the broad beans and mushrooms, cover and cook for 5–6 minutes, using the stir button occasionally until beginning to steam.
3 Add the remaining ingredients, cover, stir to mix and bring to the boil for 3–4 minutes. Reduce the heat to simmer and cook for the remaining time using the stir button occasionally. Blend to the consistency you prefer. Season to taste, if necessary.
4 Ladle or pour the piping hot soup into bowls and serve immediately.

JUG-STYLE SOUP MAKER
Thaw the broad beans if frozen. Put all the prepared ingredients (step 1 above) and other ingredients into the metal jug. Secure the lid in place. Select the chunky function and leave to cook. Blend to the consistency you prefer. Season to taste, if necessary. Serve the soup as in step 4 above.

Haricot, Pea and Broad Bean Soup

Fill a flask with this hearty soup to take on a walk or to work.

SERVES 4
1 onion
2 garlic cloves
3 tomatoes
200g can haricot beans
1 tbsp olive oil
200g (7oz) small broad beans, fresh or frozen
200g (7oz) peas, fresh or frozen
850ml (1½ pints) vegetable or chicken stock
1 tbsp Worcestershire sauce
Freshly milled black pepper, to taste
Hot naan bread, to serve

1   Finely chop the onion and garlic. Roughly chop the tomatoes.
    Drain the liquid off the haricot beans.
2   Put the oil into the glass jar. Set the timer to 30 minutes and the
    temperature to high. Add the onion and garlic, cover and cook
    for 1 minute using the stir button occasionally. Add the
    tomatoes, broad beans and peas, cover and cook for 4–5 minutes
    until steaming, using the stir button occasionally.
3   Add the remaining ingredients, cover, stir to mix and bring to
    the boil for 3–4 minutes. Reduce the heat to simmer and cook
    for the remaining time using the stir button occasionally. Blend
    to the consistency you prefer. Season to taste, if necessary.
4   Ladle or pour the piping hot soup into bowls and serve
    immediately with hot naan bread.

JUG-STYLE SOUP MAKER
Thaw the broad beans and peas if frozen. Put all the prepared
ingredients (step 1 above) and other ingredients into the metal jug.
Secure the lid in place. Select the chunky function and leave to cook.
Blend to the consistency you prefer. Season to taste, if necessary.
Serve the soup as in step 4 above.

Bean and Vegetable Soup

Turmeric adds a yellow colour and warm, spicy flavour to this winter soup.

SERVES 4
2 onions
1 garlic clove
1 carrot
1 parsnip
1 tbsp olive oil
400g (14oz) broad beans, fresh or frozen
700ml (1¼ pints) vegetable, mushroom or chicken stock
1 tsp ground turmeric
Freshly milled black pepper, to taste
Grated Parmesan or pecorino cheese, to serve

1 Roughly chop the onions and garlic then roughly chop the carrot and parsnip.
2 Put the oil into the glass jar. Set the timer to 30 minutes and the temperature to high. Add the onion and garlic, cover and cook for 3 minutes using the stir button occasionally. Add the carrot, parsnip and broad beans, cover and cook for 5–6 minutes, using the stir button occasionally until beginning to steam.
3 Add the remaining ingredients, cover, stir to mix and bring to the boil for 3–4 minutes. Reduce the heat to simmer and cook for the remaining time using the stir button occasionally. Blend to the consistency you prefer. Season to taste, if necessary.
4 Ladle or pour the piping hot soup into bowls and serve immediately with grated Parmesan or pecorino cheese to sprinkle over.

JUG-STYLE SOUP MAKER
Thaw the broad beans if frozen. Put all the prepared ingredients (step 1 above) and other ingredients into the metal jug. Secure the lid in place. Select the chunky function and leave to cook. Blend to the consistency you prefer. Season to taste if necessary. Serve the soup as in step 4 above.

Pea and Pinto Bean Soup

Pinto beans are most often used in Mexican refried beans, but make a delicious addition to a pea soup.

SERVES 4
1 onion
6 tomatoes
1 bunch of parsley
400g can pinto beans
1 tbsp olive oil
350g (12oz) peas, fresh or frozen
700ml (1¼ pints) vegetable, mushroom or chicken stock
2 tbsp tomato purée
½ tsp dried mixed herbs
Freshly milled black pepper, to taste
Wholemeal rolls, to serve

1   Finely chop the onion. Roughly chop the tomatoes. Pull the parsley leaves from the stalks and finely chop. Drain the liquid off the pinto beans.
2   Put the oil into the glass jar. Set the timer to 25 minutes and the temperature to high. Add the onion, cover and cook for 2 minutes using the stir button occasionally. Add the tomatoes and peas, cover and cook for 3–4 minutes using the stir button occasionally, until steaming.
3   Add the remaining ingredients, cover, stir to mix and bring to the boil for 1–2 minutes. Reduce the heat to simmer and cook for the remaining time using the stir button occasionally. Blend to the consistency you prefer. Season to taste, if necessary.
4   Ladle or pour the piping hot soup into bowls and serve immediately with wholemeal rolls.

JUG-STYLE SOUP MAKER
Thaw the peas if frozen. Put all the prepared ingredients (step 1 above) and other ingredients into the metal jug. Secure the lid in place. Select the chunky function and leave to cook. Blend to the consistency you prefer. Season to taste, if necessary. Serve the soup as in step 4 above.

Chilli Broad Bean and Red Pepper Soup

Chili paste adds quite a kick – for a bit of excitement, add some extra.

SERVES 4
1 onion
2 red peppers
1 sprig of thyme
1 tbsp olive oil
450g (1lb) small broad beans, fresh or frozen
700ml (1¼ pints) vegetable, mushroom or chicken stock
1 tsp chilli paste
Freshly milled black pepper, to taste

1   Roughly chop the onion. Cut the peppers in half, remove the stalk and seeds and roughly chop. Pull the thyme leaves from the stalk.
2   Put the oil into the glass jar. Set the timer to 30 minutes and the temperature to high. Add the onion, cover and cook for 2 minutes using the stir button occasionally. Add the red peppers and broad beans, cover and cook for 4–5 minutes until steaming, using the stir button occasionally.
3   Remove the lid and add the remaining ingredients, cover, stir to mix and bring to the boil for 3–4 minutes. Reduce the heat to simmer and cook for the remaining time using the stir button occasionally. Blend to the consistency you prefer. Season to taste, if necessary.
4   Ladle or pour the piping hot soup into bowls and serve immediately.

JUG-STYLE SOUP MAKER

Thaw the broad beans if frozen. Put all the prepared ingredients (step 1 above) and other ingredients into the metal jug. Secure the lid in place. Select the chunky function and leave to cook. Blend to the consistency you prefer. Season to taste, if necessary. Serve the soup as in step 4 above.

Soya Bean and Corn Chowder

This substantial soup makes a delicious meal with olive focaccia bread.

SERVES 4
1 onion
1 medium potato
1 small carrot
2 tsp plain flour
1 tbsp olive oil
300ml (½ pint) chicken or vegetable stock
400ml (14fl oz) milk
175g (6oz) soya beans, fresh or frozen
175g (6oz) sweetcorn, fresh or frozen
Freshly milled black pepper, to taste
Chopped parsley and toasted slices of olive focaccia, to serve

1 Roughly chop the onion. Chop the potato into small pieces. Slice the carrot. Mix the flour in a small bowl to a paste with a little cold water.
2 Put the oil into the glass jar. Set the timer to 30 minutes and the temperature to high. Add the onion, cover and cook for 1–2 minutes using the stir button occasionally. Add the potato and carrot, cover and cook for 4–5 minutes until it begins to steam.
3 Add the remaining ingredients, cover, stir to mix and bring to the boil for 2–3 minutes. Reduce the heat to simmer and cook for the remaining time. Blend until smooth. Season to taste, if necessary.
4 Ladle or pour the piping hot soup into bowls. Sprinkle chopped parsley on top and serve immediately with hot toasted slices of olive focaccia on the side.

JUG-STYLE SOUP MAKER
Thaw the soya beans and sweetcorn if frozen. Put all the prepared ingredients (step 1 above) and other ingredients into the metal jug. Secure the lid in place. Select the purée function and leave to cook. If necessary, season to taste. Serve as in step 4 above.

Pea-pod Soup

Young pea-pods have a natural sweetness and make a delightful summery soup.

SERVES 4
6 spring onions
1 green pepper
Large handful of sugar-snap peas
2.5cm (1in) piece of root ginger
2 tbsp olive oil
400g (14oz) petit pois peas, fresh or frozen
700ml (1¼ pints) vegetable, mushroom or chicken stock
150ml (¼ pint) unsweetened orange juice
2 tbsp low-salt tamari or soy sauce
Freshly milled black pepper, to taste
Pea shoots, to serve

1 Thinly slice the spring onions. Cut the pepper in half, remove the stalk and seeds and roughly chop. Thickly slice the sugar-snap peas. Finely grate the root ginger.
2 Put the oil into the glass jar. Set the timer to 20 minutes and the temperature to high. Add the spring onions, cover and cook for 1–2 minutes using the stir button occasionally until beginning to soften. Add the green pepper and petit pois peas, cover and cook for 4–5 minutes using the stir button occasionally, until beginning to steam.
3 Add the remaining ingredients, cover, stir to mix and bring to the boil for 2–3 minutes. Reduce the heat to simmer and cook for the remaining time using the stir button occasionally. Blend but leave chunky. Season to taste, if necessary.
4 Ladle or pour the piping hot soup into bowls and top with some pea shoots. Serve immediately.

JUG-STYLE SOUP MAKER
Thaw the petit pois peas if frozen. Put all the prepared ingredients (step 1 above) and other ingredients into the metal jug. Secure the lid in place. Select the chunky function and leave to cook. Blend to the consistency you prefer. Season to taste, if necessary. Serve the soup as in step 4 above.

Hot Bean Soup

Choose your favourite type of curry paste to use here – as hot as you dare.

SERVES 4
2 onions
1 garlic clove
2 large kale leaves
1 tbsp olive oil
200g (7oz) broad beans, fresh or frozen
250g (9oz) soya beans, fresh or frozen
850ml (1½ pints) vegetable, mushroom or chicken stock
1 tsp chilli paste
1 tbsp curry paste
Freshly milled black pepper, to taste

1   Roughly chop the onions and garlic. Remove the tough rib from the kale leaves and thinly slice the leaves.
2   Put the oil into the glass jar. Set the timer to 30 minutes and the temperature to high. Add the onion and garlic, cover and cook for 2 minutes using the stir button occasionally. Add the kale leaves, broad beans and soya beans, cover and cook for 4–5 minutes using the stir button occasionally, until steaming.
3   Add the remaining ingredients, cover, stir to mix and bring to the boil for 3–4 minutes. Reduce the heat to simmer and cook for the remaining time using the stir button occasionally. Blend to the consistency you prefer. Season to taste, if necessary.
4   Ladle or pour the piping hot soup into bowls and serve immediately.

JUG-STYLE SOUP MAKER
Thaw the broad beans and soya beans if frozen. Put all the prepared ingredients (step 1 above) and other ingredients into the metal jug. Secure the lid in place. Select the chunky function and leave to cook. Blend to the consistency you prefer. Season to taste, if necessary. Serve the soup as in step 4 above.

Celeriac, Broad Bean and Horseradish Soup

Celeriac has a thick knobbly skin which needs to be cut away before you use it.

SERVES 4
1 onion
1 piece of celeriac, about 250g (9oz)
3 sprigs of tarragon
2 tbsp olive oil
400g (14oz) broad beans, fresh or frozen
850ml (1½ pints) vegetable, mushroom or chicken stock
2–3 tsp horseradish sauce
Freshly milled black pepper, to taste
Grated Parmesan or pecorino cheese, to serve

1   Roughly chop the onion. Peel the celeriac and cut into small pieces. Pull the tarragon leaves from the stalks.
2   Put the oil into the glass jar. Set the timer to 30 minutes and the temperature to high. Add the onion, cover and cook for 2 minutes using the stir button occasionally. Add the celeriac, cover and cook for 4–5 minutes, using the stir button occasionally, until beginning to steam.
3   Add the remaining ingredients, cover, stir to mix and bring to the boil for 4–5 minutes. Reduce the heat to simmer and cook for the remaining time using the stir button occasionally. Blend to the consistency you prefer. Season to taste, if necessary.
4   Ladle or pour the piping hot soup into bowls. Sprinkle some grated cheese on top and serve immediately.

JUG-STYLE SOUP MAKER
Thaw the broad beans if frozen. Put all the prepared ingredients (step 1 above) and other ingredients into the metal jug. Secure the lid in place. Select the chunky function and leave to cook. Blend to the consistency you prefer. Season to taste, if necessary. Serve the soup as in step 4 above.

Minted Petit Pois and Broad Bean Soup

Petit pois peas have a sweet taste that goes perfectly with fresh mint.

SERVES 4
1 red onion
2 courgettes
Handful of mint leaves
1 tbsp olive oil
250g (9oz) petit pois peas, fresh or frozen
250g (9oz) small broad beans, fresh or frozen
700ml (1¼ pints) vegetable or chicken stock
Freshly milled black pepper, to taste

1 Finely chop the onion. Cut the courgettes into small pieces. Tear the mint leaves in half.
2 Put the oil into the glass jar. Set the timer to 25 minutes and the temperature to high. Add the onion, cover and cook for 1 minute using the stir button occasionally. Add the courgettes, peas and broad beans, cover and cook for 3–4 minutes using the stir button occasionally, until beginning to steam.
3 Add the remaining ingredients, cover, stir to mix and bring to the boil for 3–4 minutes. Reduce the heat to simmer and cook for the remaining time using the stir button occasionally. Blend to the consistency you prefer. Season to taste, if necessary.
4 Ladle or pour the piping hot soup into bowls and serve immediately.

JUG-STYLE SOUP MAKER
Thaw the peas and broad beans if frozen. Put all the prepared ingredients (step 1 above) and other ingredients into the metal jug. Secure the lid in place. Select the chunky function and leave to cook. Blend to the consistency you prefer. Season to taste, if necessary. Serve the soup as in step 4 above.

Flageolet, Spring Cabbage and Broccoli Soup

This soup works just as well with red cabbage or coloured Swiss chard leaves.

SERVES 4
3 shallots
250g (9oz) spring cabbage leaves
200g (7oz) broccoli spears
400g can flageolet beans
1 tbsp olive oil
700ml (1¼ pints) vegetable, mushroom or chicken stock
3 sage leaves
Freshly milled black pepper, to taste

1   Finely chop the shallots, thinly slice the cabbage leaves and cut the broccoli into small pieces. Drain the liquid off the flageolet beans.
2   Put the oil into the glass jar. Set the timer to 25 minutes and the temperature to high. Add the shallots, cover and cook for 1–2 minutes until softened, using the stir button occasionally. Add the spring cabbage and broccoli, cover and cook for 4–5 minutes until steaming, using the stir button occasionally.
3   Add the remaining ingredients, cover, stir to mix and bring to the boil for 3–4 minutes. Reduce the heat to simmer and cook for the remaining time, using the stir button occasionally. Blend to the consistency you prefer. Season to taste, if necessary.
4   Ladle or pour the piping hot soup into bowls and serve immediately.

JUG-STYLE SOUP MAKER
Put all the prepared ingredients (step 1 above) and other ingredients into the metal jug. Secure the lid in place. Select the chunky function and leave to cook. Blend to the consistency you prefer. Season to taste, if necessary. Serve the soup as in step 4 above.

Fruiting Vegetables

Fruiting vegetables are the ones which ripen and swell and grow into more or less rounded shapes. They also become highly colourful. Bright and varied colours in food are one of the key indicators of a healthy diet. So the squashes, peppers, tomatoes and aubergines – the star turns in these lively, vivid and often quite spicy soups – are a sure sign that we are happily in the world of superfoods.

Butternut Squash Soup with Toasted Pine Nuts and Chilli Pesto

There are many different types of squash available all year round – different colours and flavours – you can make this soup different every time.

SERVES 4
1 red chilli
Large handful of basil leaves
Small handful of toasted pine nuts
1 tbsp grated Parmesan cheese
4 tbsp olive oil
Sea salt and freshly milled black pepper, to taste
1 red onion
2 garlic cloves
1 carrot
600g (1lb 5oz) wedge of butternut squash
700ml (1¼ pints) vegetable or chicken stock
Hot crusty bread, to serve

1   Start by making the pesto. Cut the chilli in half, remove the stalk and seeds and finely chop. Whizz together the chilli, basil leaves, half of the pine nuts, grated Parmesan cheese, 2 tablespoons of the oil and a little seasoning. Spoon into a small bowl and chill until later.
2   Roughly chop the onion and garlic. Slice the carrot. Remove any seeds from the butternut squash, peel and cut into small cubes.
3   Put the oil into the glass jar. Set the timer to 30 minutes and the temperature to high. Add the onion and garlic, cover and cook for 1–2 minutes using the stir button occasionally until they begin to steam, but without browning too much. Add the stock, cover and cook for 5–6 minutes until steaming, using the stir button occasionally.

4 Add the remaining ingredients, cover, stir to mix and bring to the boil. Reduce the heat to simmer and cook for the remaining time using the stir button occasionally. Blend to the consistency you prefer. Season to taste, if necessary.
5 Ladle or pour the piping hot soup into bowls. Scatter over the remaining toasted pine nuts and add a swirl of the pesto. Serve immediately with hot crusty bread.

JUG-STYLE SOUP MAKER

Prepare the pesto (step 1 above) and chill until later. Put all the prepared ingredients (step 2 above) and other ingredients into the metal jug. Secure the lid in place. Select the purée function and leave to cook. Season to taste, if necessary. Serve the soup as in step 5 above.

Courgette, Tomato and Pea Soup

I like using whole spices like the fennel seeds used here. They become crushed as the soup is blended but use ground if you prefer a smoother taste. In a hot pan lightly dry-fry whole seeds for a few seconds for extra flavour.

SERVES 4
2 onions
250g (9oz) ripe tomatoes
4 courgettes
250g (9oz) peas, fresh or frozen
2 tbsp sunflower oil
850ml (1½ pints) chicken or vegetable stock
1 tsp fennel seeds
Freshly milled black pepper, to taste

1   Finely chop the onions. Roughly chop the tomatoes removing any tough cores. Slice the courgettes.
2   Put the oil into the glass jar. Set the timer to 20 minutes and the temperature to high. Add the onion, cover and cook for 1–2 minutes using the stir button occasionally until beginning to steam, but without browning too much. Add the courgettes, cover and cook for 3–4 minutes using the stir button occasionally until beginning to steam.
3   Add the remaining ingredients, cover, stir to mix and bring to the boil. Reduce the heat to simmer and cook for the remaining time using the stir button occasionally. Leave the soup chunky or blend to the consistency you prefer. Season to taste, if necessary.
4   Ladle or pour the piping hot soup into bowls and serve immediately.

JUG-STYLE SOUP MAKER
Put all the prepared ingredients (step 1 above) and other ingredients into the metal jug. Secure the lid in place. Select the chunky function and leave to cook. Season to taste, if necessary. Blend to the consistency you prefer. Serve as in step 4 above.

Tomato and Bean Soup with Ricotta Cheese

This classic combination is always a favourite soup.

SERVES 4
1 onion
300g (10½oz) mixed long green beans
Small bunch of basil leaves
2 tbsp olive oil
700ml (1¼ pints) chicken or vegetable stock
400g can tomatoes
2 tbsp tomato purée
Freshly milled black pepper, to taste

TOPPING
4 slices of sourdough bread
Ricotta cheese, for spreading

1   Finely chop the onion. Top and tail the beans and cut into small chunks. Pull the basil leaves from the stalks.
2   Put the oil into the glass jar. Set the timer to 20 minutes and the temperature to high. Add the onion, cover and cook for 1–2 minutes, using the stir button occasionally until beginning to soften. Add the beans, cover and cook for 2–3 minutes until steaming, using the stir button occasionally.
3   Add the remaining ingredients, cover, stir to mix and bring to the boil for a minute, then reduce the heat to simmer and cook for the remaining time, using the stir button occasionally. Blend to the consistency you prefer. Season to taste, if necessary.
4   While the soup is cooking, make the topping. Toast the bread on both sides under a hot grill. Spread ricotta cheese on top of each slice. Put back under the hot grill until heated through.
5   Ladle or pour the piping hot soup into bowls. Put a cheese toast on top of each bowl. Serve immediately.

JUG-STYLE SOUP MAKER
Put all the prepared ingredients (step 1 above) and other ingredients into the metal jug. Secure the lid in place. Select the chunky function and leave to cook. Season the soup to taste, if necessary. While the soup is cooking make the topping (see step 4) above. Season the soup to taste, if necessary, and serve as in step 5 above.

Chilled Cucumber and Watercress Soup

Don't just save this for summer: chilled soups are refreshing at any time of the year.

SERVES 4
2 shallots
2 cucumbers
1 large potato
1 bunch of watercress
2–3 tarragon sprigs
1 tbsp sunflower oil
700ml (1¼ pints) vegetable stock
150ml (¼ pint) natural yogurt
Freshly milled black pepper, to taste
Watercress leaves, to serve

1   Finely chop the shallots. Cut the cucumbers in half lengthways, scoop out the seeds and roughly chop. Cut the potato into small pieces. Roughly chop the watercress discarding any strong stems. Pull the tarragon leaves from the stalks.
2   Put the oil into the glass jar. Set the timer to 25 minutes and the temperature to high. Add the chopped shallots, cover and cook for 2–3 minutes, using the stir button occasionally until just lightly browned and starting to soften. Add the potato, cover and cook for 4–5 minutes, using the stir button occasionally until beginning to steam.
3   Add the remaining ingredients except for the yogurt, cover, stir to mix and bring to the boil. Reduce the heat to simmer and cook for the remaining time using the stir button occasionally. Pour in the yogurt, cover and blend until smooth. Season to taste, if necessary.
4   Ladle or pour the soup into a large bowl, leave to cool and chill until required. Serve in bowls with a few watercress leaves scattered over.

JUG-STYLE SOUP MAKER
Put all the prepared ingredients (step 1 above) and other ingredients, except the yogurt, into the metal jug. Secure the lid in place. Select the purée function and leave to cook. Stir in the yogurt. Season to taste, if necessary. See step 4 above for chilling and serving the soup.

Pumpkin and Sweet Potato Soup

The starchy pumpkin and sweet potato help to thicken this velvety soup.

SERVES 4
1 red onion
2 garlic cloves
450g (1lb) wedge of pumpkin
1 small sweet potato
2 tbsp olive oil
2.5cm (1in) piece of root ginger
¼ tsp ground allspice
Freshly milled black pepper, to taste
850ml (1½ pints) chicken or vegetable stock

1   Finely chop the onion and garlic. Remove any seeds from the pumpkin, peel and cut into small cubes. Cut the sweet potato into small pieces.
2   Put the oil into the glass jar. Set the timer to 30 minutes and the temperature to high. Add the onion and garlic, cover and cook for 1–2 minutes using the stir button occasionally until they begin to steam but without browning too much. Add the pumpkin and sweet potato, cover and cook for 5–6 minutes until steaming, using the stir button occasionally.
3   Add the remaining ingredients, cover, stir to mix and bring to the boil. Reduce the heat to simmer and cook for the remaining time, using the stir button occasionally. Blend to the consistency you prefer. Season to taste, if necessary.
4   Ladle or pour the piping hot soup into bowls. Serve immediately.

JUG-STYLE SOUP MAKER
Put all the prepared ingredients (step 1 above) and other ingredients into the metal jug. Secure the lid in place. Select the purée function and leave to cook. Season to taste, if necessary. Serve the soup as in step 4 above.

Aubergine Soup with Harissa and Sesame Seeds

Harissa paste is great for flavouring soups – it's made with chillies, garlic, cumin, coriander and caraway.

SERVES 4
1 red onion
2 garlic cloves
1 large aubergine
6 sun-dried tomatoes
2 tbsp olive oil
700ml (1¼ pints) chicken or vegetable stock
1–2 tsp harissa paste
Freshly milled black pepper, to taste
TOPPING
2 tbsp toasted sesame seeds
2 tbsp olive oil
4 tbsp chopped coriander leaves

1 Finely chop the onion and garlic. Trim the stalk from the aubergine and cut into small pieces. Finely chop the sun-dried tomatoes.
2 Put the oil into the glass jar. Set the timer to 20 minutes and the temperature to high. Add the onion and garlic, cover and cook for 1 minute, using the stir button occasionally. Add the aubergine, cover and cook for 4–5 minutes until steaming, using the stir button occasionally.
3 Add the remaining ingredients, cover, stir to mix and bring to the boil, then reduce the heat to simmer and cook for the remaining time, using the stir button occasionally. Blend to the consistency you prefer.

4 While the soup is cooking, mix all the topping ingredients together in a small bowl. Season to taste, if necessary.

5 Ladle or pour the piping hot soup into bowls. Drizzle some of the topping over each bowl. Serve immediately.

JUG-STYLE SOUP MAKER

Put all the prepared ingredients (step 1 above) and other ingredients into the metal jug. Secure the lid in place. Select the chunky function and leave to cook. While the soup is cooking, make the topping (see step 4 above). Blend the soup to the consistency you prefer. Season to taste, if necessary. Serve as in step 5 above.

Red Curry, Tomato and Mushroom Soup with Noodles

The noodles make this soup a meal in itself.

SERVES 4
1 large red onion
3 garlic cloves
1 medium red pepper
450g (1lb) ripe tomatoes
250g (9oz) button mushrooms
2 tbsp olive oil
700ml (1¼ pints) chicken or vegetable stock
1 tsp tomato purée
2 tsp curry powder, choose your favourite
½ tsp paprika pepper
Pinch of sugar
Freshly milled black pepper, to taste
300g packet of ready-cooked egg noodles
Poppadums, to serve

1   Finely chop the onion and garlic. Cut the red pepper in half, remove the stalks and seeds and thinly slice. Roughly chop the tomatoes removing any tough cores. Slice the mushrooms.
2   Put the oil into the glass jar. Set the timer to 20 minutes and the temperature to high. Add the onion and garlic, cover and cook for 1 minute, using the stir button occasionally. Add the red pepper and mushrooms, cover and cook for 4 minutes until steaming, using the stir button occasionally.

3   Add the remaining ingredients, except the noodles, cover, stir to mix and bring to the boil, then reduce the heat to simmer and cook for 10 minutes using the stir button occasionally. Add the noodles and cook for the remaining time. Season to taste, if necessary.

4   Ladle or pour the piping hot soup into bowls. Serve immediately with poppadums.

JUG-STYLE SOUP MAKER

Put all the prepared ingredients (step 1 above) and other ingredients except the noodles into the metal jug. Secure the lid in place. Select the chunky function and leave to cook. While the soup is cooking, cook the noodles following the packet instructions. Season the soup to taste, if necessary. Heap the piping hot noodles into bowls and ladle or pour the piping hot soup over. Serve as in step 4 above.

Three Pepper Soup

There is a surprise to this soup – the padron peppers. Most have a mild flavour, but a few are very hot. There's no telling until you taste the soup.

SERVES 4

1 large red onion
2 garlic cloves
3 large sweet peppers, yellow, red and orange
1 red chilli pepper
6 padron peppers
2 pak choi
4 sprigs of oregano
2 tbsp olive oil
700ml (1¼ pints) chicken or vegetable stock
150ml (¼ pint) unsweetened orange juice
Freshly milled black pepper, to taste
Slices of hot olive focaccia bread, to serve

1   Finely chop the onion and crush the garlic. Cut each of the sweet peppers and the red chilli in half, remove the stalks and seeds and roughly chop. Trim the stalks off the padron peppers and cut each into quarters. Thinly slice the pak choi. Pull the oregano leaves from the stalks.

2   Put the oil into the glass jar. Set the timer to 20 minutes and the temperature to high. Add the onion and garlic, cover and cook for 2 minutes, using the stir button occasionally until starting to soften. Add the sweet peppers, chilli and padron peppers, cover and cook for 4 minutes until steaming, using the stir button occasionally.

3   Add the remaining ingredients, cover, stir to mix and bring to the boil for a minute, then reduce the heat to simmer and cook for the remaining time, using the stir button occasionally.

4   Blend the soup to the consistency you prefer. Season to taste, if
    necessary.
5   Ladle or spoon the piping hot soup into bowls. Serve
    immediately with slices of hot olive focaccia bread.

JUG-STYLE SOUP MAKER
Put all the prepared ingredients (step 1 above) and other ingredients,
into the metal jug. Secure the lid in place. Select the purée function
and leave to cook. Season to taste, if necessary. Serve the soup as in
step 5 above.

Chilled Courgette, Tomato and Apple Soup

I like to add a few cooked, shelled prawns to the cooled soup.

SERVES 4

1 onion
4 courgettes
2 celery sticks with leaves
1 cooking apple
1 tbsp olive oil
700ml (1¼ pints) vegetable stock
150ml (¼ pint) tomato juice
Freshly milled black pepper, to taste
Toasted sunflower seeds and extra celery leaves, to serve

1   Finely chop the onion. Cut the courgettes into small pieces.
    Thinly slice the celery and leaves. Peel, core and roughly chop
    the apple.
2   Put the oil into the glass jar. Set the timer to 25 minutes and the
    temperature to high. Add the chopped onion, cover and cook for
    1–2 minutes, using the stir button occasionally, until just lightly
    browned and starting to soften. Add the courgettes and celery,
    cover and cook for 4–5 minutes, using the stir button
    occasionally until beginning to steam.
3   Add the remaining ingredients, cover, stir to mix and bring to
    the boil for 2 minutes. Reduce the heat to simmer and cook for
    the remaining time using the stir button occasionally. Blend
    until smooth. Season to taste, if necessary.
4   Ladle or pour the soup into a large bowl, leave to cool and chill
    until required. Serve in bowls topped with a few toasted
    sunflower seeds and celery leaves.

JUG-STYLE SOUP MAKER

Put all the prepared ingredients (step 1 above) and other ingredients,
into the metal jug. Secure the lid in place. Select the purée function
and leave to cook. Season to taste, if necessary. See step 4 above for
chilling and serving the soup.

Aubergine and Red Pepper Soup

Aubergine is an unusual ingredient in soups, but gives a lovely creamy texture.

SERVES 4
1 onion
2 garlic cloves
1 large aubergine
1 large red pepper
4 sprigs of thyme
2 tbsp olive oil
850ml (1½ pints) chicken or vegetable stock
1 tsp smoked paprika pepper
Freshly milled black pepper, to taste

1   Finely chop the onion and garlic. Trim the stalk from the aubergine and cut into small pieces. Cut the pepper in half, remove the stalk and seeds and roughly chop. Pull the thyme leaves from the stalks.
2   Put the oil into the glass jar. Set the timer to 20 minutes and the temperature to high. Add the onion and garlic, cover and cook for 1 minute, using the stir button occasionally. Add the aubergine, cover and cook for 4–5 minutes until steaming, using the stir button occasionally.
3   Add the remaining ingredients, cover, stir to mix and bring to the boil, then reduce the heat to simmer and cook for the remaining time, using the stir button occasionally. Blend to the consistency you prefer. Season to taste, if necessary.
4   Ladle or pour the piping hot soup into bowls. Serve immediately.

JUG-STYLE SOUP MAKER
Put all the prepared ingredients (step 1 above) and other ingredients into the metal jug. Secure the lid in place. Select the chunky function and leave to cook. Blend the soup to the consistency you prefer. Season to taste, if necessary. Serve as in step 4 above.

Courgette, Green Pepper and Rice Soup

Brown rice gives a nutty flavour to this soup.

SERVES 4
1 onion
4 courgettes
2 green peppers
Small bunch of flat-leafed parsley
6 stoned black olives
2 tbsp olive oil
400ml (14fl oz) chicken or vegetable stock
300ml (½ pint) milk
1 tbsp lemon juice
Half a 250g packet of cooked brown rice
Freshly milled black pepper, to taste
3 tbsp natural yogurt or single cream, to serve

1 Finely chop the onion. Thinly slice the courgettes. Cut the
   peppers in half, remove the stalks and seeds and roughly chop.
   Pull the parsley leaves from the stalks. Thinly slice the olives.
2 Put the oil into the glass jar. Set the timer to 30 minutes and the
   temperature to high. Add the onion, cover and cook for
   2 minutes, using the stir button occasionally until beginning to
   soften. Add the courgettes and peppers, cover and cook for
   3–4 minutes until steaming, using the stir button occasionally.

3 Add the remaining ingredients except the rice and sliced olives. Cover, stir to mix and bring to the boil for a minute, then reduce the heat to simmer and cook for 20 minutes, using the stir button occasionally. Add the cooked rice and sliced olives and cook for the remaining time. Stir in the yogurt or cream. Season to taste, if necessary.

4 Ladle or pour the piping hot soup into bowls. Serve immediately.

JUG-STYLE SOUP MAKER
Put all the prepared ingredients except the sliced olives (step 1 above) and other ingredients except the rice, into the metal jug. Secure the lid in place. Select the chunky function and leave to cook. Season the soup to taste, if necessary. Heat the rice in the microwave until it is piping hot then stir into the soup with the yogurt or cream. Serve as in step 4 above.

Chilli Red Pepper Soup

Top this colourful, spicy soup with crunchy toasted breadcrumbs before you serve.

SERVES 4
1 red onion
1 garlic clove
2 large red peppers
1 red chilli
4 sprigs of oregano
2 tbsp olive oil
300ml (½ pint) passata
700ml (1¼ pints) chicken or vegetable stock
½ tsp ground cumin
½ tsp ground coriander
Pinch of sugar
Freshly milled black pepper, to taste
Toasted breadcrumbs, to serve

1   Finely chop the onion and crush the garlic. Cut the red peppers and the chilli in half, remove the stalks and seeds and roughly chop. Pull the oregano leaves from the stalks.
2   Put the oil into the glass jar. Set the timer to 20 minutes and the temperature to high. Add the onion and garlic, cover and cook for 2 minutes, using the stir button occasionally. Add the red pepper and chilli, cover and cook for 5 minutes until steaming, using the stir button occasionally.
3   Add the remaining ingredients, cover, stir to mix and bring to the boil, then reduce the heat to simmer and cook for the remaining time, using the stir button occasionally.

4 Blend the soup to the consistency you prefer. Season to taste, if necessary.

5 Ladle or spoon the piping hot soup into bowls and scatter over a few toasted breadcrumbs. Serve immediately.

JUG-STYLE SOUP MAKER

Put all the prepared ingredients (step 1 above) and other ingredients, into the metal jug. Secure the lid in place. Select the chunky function and leave to cook. Leave chunky or blend as you prefer. Season to taste, if necessary. Serve the soup as in step 5 above.

French Bean Soup

This is a very simple soup to make.

SERVES 4
4 shallots
2 garlic cloves
500g (1lb 2oz) French long green beans
1 sweet potato
2 tbsp olive oil
700ml (1¼ pints) chicken or vegetable stock
Freshly milled black pepper, to taste
Hot crusty bread, to serve

1   Finely chop the shallots and garlic. Top and tail the beans and
    cut into small chunks. Cut the sweet potato into small pieces.
2   Put the oil into the glass jar. Set the timer to 20 minutes and the
    temperature to high. Add the shallots and garlic, cover and cook
    for 1–2 minutes, using the stir button occasionally, until
    beginning to soften. Add the sweet potato and beans, cover and
    cook for 4 minutes until steaming, using the stir button
    occasionally.
3   Add the remaining ingredients, cover, stir to mix and bring to
    the boil for a minute, then reduce the heat to simmer and cook
    for the remaining time, using the stir button occasionally. Blend
    to the consistency you prefer. Season to taste, if necessary.
4   Ladle or pour the piping hot soup into bowls. Serve immediately
    with hot crusty bread.

JUG-STYLE SOUP MAKER
Put all the prepared ingredients (step 1 above) and other ingredients
into the metal jug. Secure the lid in place. Select the chunky function
and leave to cook. Season the soup to taste, if necessary. Serve as in
step 4 above.

Roasted Tomato, Pepper and Squash Soup

Roasting the vegetables beforehand gives a hint of a barbecue taste to the soup.

SERVES 4

1 large red onion
6 Italian tomatoes (such as San Marzano)
1 green pepper
280g (10oz) wedge of butternut squash
2 tbsp olive oil
½ tsp dried mixed herbs
Freshly milled black pepper, to taste
700ml (1¼ pints) vegetable or chicken stock
Hot, torn pieces of flatbread, to serve

1   Preheat the oven to 200°C, fan 180°C, gas 6.
2   Cut the onion into eight wedges. Quarter the tomatoes. Cut the pepper in half, remove the stalk and seeds and cut each half into four pieces. Remove any seeds from the butternut squash, peel and roughly cut into small pieces.
3   Arrange the vegetables in a roasting tin and drizzle over the olive oil. Put into the hot oven and cook for about 10–15 minutes until golden.
4   Put the roasted vegetables with any juices into the glass jar. Set the timer to 20 minutes and the temperature to high. Add the remaining ingredients. Cover, stir to mix and bring to the boil. Reduce the heat to simmer and cook for the remaining time, using the stir button occasionally. Blend to the consistency you prefer. Season to taste, if necessary.
5   Ladle or pour the piping hot soup into bowls. Serve immediately with hot torn pieces of flatbread.

JUG-STYLE SOUP MAKER

Put all the prepared ingredients (steps 1–3 above) and other ingredients into the metal jug. Secure the lid in place. Select the purée function and leave to cook. Season to taste, if necessary. Serve the soup as in step 5 above.

Bean-Feast Soup with Chestnuts and Rosemary

Chestnuts add a rich flavour to this soup. They are available all year round: frozen, vacuum packed or in tins.

SERVES 4
1 small leek
200g (7oz) runner beans
200g (7oz) long round green beans
200g (7oz) fine green beans
1 sprig of rosemary
8 cooked chestnuts, frozen or vacuum packed
2 tbsp olive oil
700ml (1¼ pints) chicken or vegetable stock
Freshly milled black pepper, to taste

1   Finely chop the leek. Top and tail all the beans and cut into small chunks. Pull the rosemary leaves from the woody stalk. Roughly chop the chestnuts.
2   Put the oil into the glass jar. Set the timer to 20 minutes and the temperature to high. Add the leek, cover and cook for 2–3 minutes, using the stir button occasionally, until beginning to soften. Add the beans, cover and cook for 3–4 minutes until steaming, using the stir button occasionally.
3   Add the remaining ingredients, cover, stir to mix and bring to the boil for a minute, then reduce the heat to simmer and cook for the remaining time, using the stir button occasionally. Blend to the consistency you prefer. Season to taste, if necessary.
4   Ladle or pour the piping hot soup into bowls. Serve immediately.

JUG-STYLE SOUP MAKER
Thaw the chestnuts if frozen. Put all the prepared ingredients (step 1 above) and other ingredients into the metal jug. Secure the lid in place. Select the chunky function and leave to cook. Season the soup to taste, if necessary. Serve as in step 4 above.

Sea Fish and Shellfish

Oily fish, white fish, meaty fish and shellfish – all of them contain so much goodness that we should be eating fish two or three times a week, if not more. Fish soups are a lovely way to thrive and derive benefit from this rich nutritious source, and with a wide range of other superfoods included in these recipes as well, these delicious, evocative soups – full of the flavours of the sea – should become firm favourites to return to again and again. Always cook fish and shellfish before using them in a jug-style soup maker.

Salmon and Watercress Soup

Fennel and watercress add interesting aniseed and peppery flavours.

SERVES 4
1 onion
1 fennel bulb
1 potato
1 small lemon
2 bunches of watercress
450g (1lb) skinless salmon fillet
1 tbsp olive oil
300ml (½ pint) fish stock
300ml (½ pint) vegetable or chicken stock
Freshly milled black pepper, to taste
Watercress leaves and natural yogurt, to serve

1   Finely chop the onion. Thinly slice the fennel. Cut the potato
    into small pieces. Cut the lemon in half and squeeze out the
    juice. Pull the watercress leaves from the stalks. Remove any
    bones from the salmon fillet and cut into bite-sized pieces.
2   Put the oil into the glass jar. Set the timer to 30 minutes and the
    temperature to high. Add the onion, cover and cook for 1 minute
    using the stir button occasionally until beginning to brown a
    little. Add the fennel and potato, cover and cook for 5 minutes
    using the stir button occasionally until beginning to steam.

3   Add the remaining ingredients except the salmon pieces. Cover, stir to mix and bring just up to the boil. Immediately reduce the heat to simmer and cook for the remaining time, using the stir button occasionally. 10–15 minutes before the end of the cooking time stir the salmon pieces into the soup and simmer until cooked through. Blend to the consistency you prefer. Season to taste, if necessary.
4   Ladle or pour the piping hot soup into bowls. Top with a swirl of yogurt and a few watercress leaves. Serve immediately.

JUG-STYLE SOUP MAKER

Remove any bones from the salmon fillet. Cut into bite-sized pieces and poach in a little stock until cooked. Put all the prepared ingredients except the salmon (step 1 above) and other ingredients into the metal jug. Secure the lid in place. Select the chunky function and leave to cook. 6–8 minutes before the end of the cooking time stir the salmon pieces into the soup, cover and continue cooking. Season to taste, if necessary. Serve the soup as in step 4 above.

Prawn and Clam Soup

If you've bought clams in their shells, put them into a hot pan with a little stock or water. Cover and cook for a minute or two and they'll steam open.

SERVES 4
1 onion
Small bunch of coriander
2 courgettes
1 tbsp olive oil
1 tbsp lemon juice
150g (5½oz) peas
400ml (14fl oz) fish or vegetable stock
300ml (½ pint) chicken or vegetable stock
Freshly milled black pepper, to taste
200g (7oz) cooked, peeled prawns
200g (7oz) cooked, shelled clams
Coriander leaves, to serve

1   Finely chop the onion. Pull the coriander leaves from the stalks and finely chop. Finely chop the courgettes.
2   Put the oil into the glass jar. Set the timer to 20 minutes and the temperature to high. Add the onion, cover and cook for 1–2 minutes until steaming, using the stir button occasionally. Add the courgettes, cover and cook for 3–4 minutes until steaming, using the stir button occasionally.

3   Add the remaining ingredients except the prawns and clams. Cover, stir to mix and bring to the boil, then reduce the heat to simmer and cook for 10 minutes, using the stir button occasionally. 4–6 minutes before the end of the cooking time stir the prawns and clams into the soup and simmer until cooked through. Blend to the consistency you prefer. Season to taste, if necessary.
4   Ladle or spoon the piping hot soup into bowls. Top with coriander leaves and serve immediately.

JUG-STYLE SOUP MAKER
Thaw the prawns, clams or peas, if frozen. Put all the prepared ingredients (step 1 above) and the other ingredients except the prawns and clams into the metal jug. Secure the lid in place. Select the chunky function and leave to cook. 4–6 minutes before the end of the cooking time stir the prawns and clams into the soup, cover and continue cooking. Season to taste, if necessary. Serve the soup as in step 4.

Smoked Haddock Soup

Lightly smoked fish gives a tangy flavour. I always prefer to use undyed haddock.

SERVES 4
1 onion
1 small lemon
3 large handfuls of small spinach leaves
350g (12 oz) skinless undyed smoked haddock fillet
1 tbsp olive oil
400ml (14fl oz) fish or vegetable stock
300ml (½ pint) vegetable or chicken stock
Freshly milled black pepper, to taste
Seeded rolls, to serve

1   Finely chop the onion. Cut the lemon in half and squeeze out the juice. Roughly chop the spinach leaves. Remove any bones from the haddock and cut into bite-sized pieces.
2   Put the oil into the glass jar. Set the timer to 25 minutes and the temperature to high. Add the onion, cover and cook for 1–2 minutes, using the stir button occasionally, until beginning to soften. Add the spinach, cover and cook for 1–2 minutes, using the stir button occasionally, until beginning to steam.
3   Add the remaining ingredients except the smoked haddock. Cover, stir to mix and bring just up to the boil. Immediately reduce the heat to simmer and cook for the remaining time using the stir button occasionally. 6–8 minutes before the end of the cooking time stir the pieces of smoked haddock into the soup and simmer until cooked through. Blend to the consistency you prefer. Season to taste, if necessary.

4 Ladle or pour the piping hot soup into bowls and serve immediately with seeded rolls.

JUG-STYLE SOUP MAKER
Remove any bones from the smoked haddock. Cut into bite-sized pieces and poach in a little stock until cooked.. Put all the prepared ingredients except the haddock pieces (step 1 above) and other ingredients into the metal jug. Secure the lid in place. Select the chunky function and leave to cook. 6–8 minutes before the end of the cooking time stir the pieces of smoked haddock into the soup, cover and continue cooking. Season to taste, if necessary. Serve the soup as in step 4.

Trout, Prawn and Chard Soup

Hot smoking of fish cooks it so it only needs to be added at the end of the cooking time to heat through.

SERVES 4
1 red onion
1 small orange
3 large handfuls of small Swiss chard leaves
2 hot smoked trout fillets
1 tbsp olive oil
300ml (½ pint) fish or vegetable stock
300ml (½ pint) vegetable or chicken stock
Freshly milled black pepper, to taste
140g (5oz) cooked, shelled prawns

1 Finely chop the onion. Cut the orange in half and squeeze out the juice. Roughly chop the chard leaves. Remove any skin and bones from the trout fillets and cut into bite-sized pieces.
2 Put the oil into the glass jar. Set the timer to 25 minutes and the temperature to high. Add the onion, cover and cook for 1–2 minutes, using the stir button occasionally, until beginning to soften. Add the Swiss chard leaves, cover and cook for 1–2 minutes, using the stir button occasionally, until beginning to steam.
3 Add the remaining ingredients except the trout pieces. Cover, stir to mix and bring just up to the boil. Immediately reduce the heat to simmer and cook for the remaining time, using the stir button occasionally. 4–6 minutes before the end of the cooking time stir the trout pieces and prawns into the soup and simmer until heated through. Blend to the consistency you prefer. Season to taste, if necessary.

4 Ladle or pour the piping hot soup into bowls and serve immediately.

JUG-STYLE SOUP MAKER

Remove any skin and bones from the trout fillets and cut into bite-sized pieces. Put all the prepared ingredients except the trout pieces (step 1 above) and other ingredients into the metal jug. Secure the lid in place. Select the chunky function and leave to cook. 4–6 minutes before the end of the cooking time, stir the trout pieces and prawns into the soup, cover and continue cooking. Season to taste, if necessary. Serve the soup as in step 4 above.

Red Snapper Soup with Gooseberry Salsa

No red snapper? Salmon makes a good alternative.

SERVES 4

TOPPING
100g (3½oz) gooseberries, fresh or frozen
½ tsp sugar
½ small red pepper
1 red chilli
3 tomatoes
SOUP
1 red onion
1 lime
2 pak choi
Small bunch of flat-leafed parsley
350g (12oz) skinless red snapper fillets
1 tbsp olive oil
700ml (1¼ pints) fish, vegetable or chicken stock
Freshly milled black pepper, to taste
Croûtons, to serve

1   Make the salsa beforehand. Put the gooseberries, sugar and a
    little water into a small pan. Bring to the boil and cook until soft
    and most of the liquid has evaporated. Spoon into a small bowl
    and leave until cold.
2   Remove the stalk and seeds from the red pepper. Cut the chilli
    in half, remove the stalk and seeds. Finely chop the pepper and
    chilli. Quarter the tomatoes, remove the cores and finely chop.
    Stir the pepper, chilli and tomatoes into the cooked
    gooseberries, cover and chill.
3   To make the soup, finely chop the onion, cut the lime in half and
    squeeze out the juice. Finely chop the pak choi. Pull the parsley
    leaves off the stalks and finely chop. Remove any bones from the
    red snapper fillets and cut into bite-sized pieces.

4 Put the oil into the glass jar. Set the timer to 25 minutes and the temperature to high. Add the onion, cover and cook for 1–2 minutes, using the stir button occasionally until beginning to brown a little. Add the pak choi, cover and cook for 4–5 minutes, using the stir button occasionally until beginning to steam.

5 Add the remaining ingredients except the salsa and the red snapper pieces. Cover, stir to mix and bring just up to the boil. Immediately reduce the heat to simmer and cook for the remaining time using the stir button occasionally. 10–15 minutes before the end of the cooking time stir the red snapper pieces into the soup and simmer until cooked through. Blend to the consistency you prefer. Season to taste, if necessary.

6 Ladle or pour the piping hot soup into bowls. Sprinkle a few croûtons on top of the soup and add a spoonful of the gooseberry salsa or serve it on the side. Serve immediately.

JUG-STYLE SOUP MAKER

Remove any bones from the red snapper fillet. Cut into bite-sized pieces and poach in a little stock until cooked. Prepare the salsa as in steps 1 and 2. Put all the prepared ingredients (step 3), except the fish pieces and the salsa, and the other ingredients into the metal jug. Secure the lid in place. Select the chunky function and leave to cook. 6–8 minutes before the end of the cooking time stir the red snapper pieces into the soup, cover and continue cooking. Season to taste, if necessary. Serve the soup as in step 6 above.

Coconut, Lime and Fish Soup

You can often find mixed pieces of fish for sale at the fish counter: ideal for soups or pies.

SERVES 4

1 onion

2 garlic cloves

1 lime

4 large handfuls of spinach leaves

500g (1lb 2oz) mixed skinless fish pieces such as
   salmon, whiting, haddock or trout

1 tbsp olive oil

300ml (½ pint) fish, vegetable or chicken stock

400ml can coconut milk

¼ tsp ground turmeric

Freshly milled black pepper, to taste

Hot tomato bread, to serve

1   Finely chop the onion and garlic. Cut the lime in half and
    squeeze out the juice. Roughly chop the spinach leaves. Remove
    any bones from the fish and cut into bite-sized pieces.

2   Put the oil into the glass jar. Set the timer to 25 minutes and the
    temperature to high. Add the onion and garlic, cover and cook
    for 1–2 minutes, using the stir button occasionally, until
    beginning to brown a little. Add the spinach, cover and cook for
    1–2 minutes, using the stir button occasionally, until beginning
    to steam.

3   Add the remaining ingredients except the fish pieces, cover, stir
    to mix and bring just up to the boil. Immediately reduce the heat
    to simmer and cook for the remaining time, using the stir button
    occasionally. 10–15 minutes before the end of the cooking time
    stir the pieces of fish into the soup and simmer until cooked
    through. Blend to the consistency you prefer. Season to taste, if
    necessary.

4 Ladle or pour the piping hot soup into bowls and serve immediately with hot tomato bread.

JUG-STYLE SOUP MAKER
Remove any bones from the fish. Cut into bite-sized pieces and poach in a little stock until cooked. Put all the prepared ingredients except the fish pieces (step 1 above) and other ingredients into the metal jug. Secure the lid in place. Select the chunky function and leave to cook. 6–8 minutes before the end of the cooking time stir the mixed fish pieces into the soup, cover and continue cooking. Season to taste, if necessary. Serve the soup as in step 4 above.

Shellfish and Saffron Soup

Saffron adds a wonderful colour and delicate flavour to this soup.

SERVES 4

1 red onion
1 garlic clove
1 carrot
400g (14oz) mixed cooked and shelled shellfish such as
    crab, cockles, shrimps, prawns, clams or mussels
1 tbsp olive oil
700ml (1¼ pints) fish, vegetable or chicken stock
300g (10½oz) leafy stir-fry mix
2 tbsp lemon juice
A good pinch of saffron threads
Freshly milled black pepper, to taste
Lemon wedges, to serve

1   Finely chop the onion and garlic. Cut the carrot into small
    pieces. Check the shellfish for any pieces of shell and cut any
    large pieces of shellfish into bite-sized portions.
2   Put the oil into the glass jar. Set the timer to 20 minutes and the
    temperature to high. Add the onion and garlic, cover and cook
    for 1–2 minutes, using the stir button occasionally, until
    beginning to brown a little. Add the leafy stir-fry mix, cover and
    cook for 1–2 minutes, using the stir button occasionally, until
    beginning to steam.
3   Add the remaining ingredients except the mixed shellfish.
    Cover, stir to mix and bring just up to the boil. Immediately
    reduce the heat to simmer and cook for the remaining time,
    using the stir button occasionally. 6–8 minutes before the end of
    the cooking time stir the mixed shellfish into the soup and
    simmer until heated through. Blend to the consistency you
    prefer. Season to taste, if necessary.

4 Ladle or pour the piping hot soup into bowls and serve immediately with lemon wedges to squeeze over.

JUG-STYLE SOUP MAKER
Put all the prepared ingredients except the mixed, cooked shellfish (step 1 above) and other ingredients into the metal jug. Secure the lid in place. Select the chunky function and leave to cook. 6–8 minutes before the end of the cooking time stir the shellfish pieces into the soup, cover and continue cooking. Season to taste, if necessary. Serve the soup as in step 4 above.

Salmon and Smoked Haddock Chowder

I've used salmon and haddock here, but try trout and pollack for a different combination.

SERVES 4
1 onion
1 large handful spinach leaves
1 medium potato
2 tsp plain flour
1 sprig of thyme
200g (7oz) skinless salmon fillet
200g (7oz) skinless smoked haddock fillet
1 tbsp olive oil
300ml (½ pint) fish, vegetable or chicken stock
400ml (14fl oz) milk
150g (5½oz) sweetcorn, fresh or frozen
1 tsp ground turmeric
Freshly milled black pepper, to taste
Hot crusty bread, to serve

1   Finely chop the onion. Roughly chop the spinach leaves. Chop the potato into small pieces. Mix the flour in a small bowl to a paste with a little cold water. Pull the thyme leaves from the stalk. Remove any bones from the salmon and haddock and cut into bite-sized pieces.
2   Put the oil into the glass jar. Set the timer to 30 minutes and the temperature to high. Add the onion, cover and cook for 1–2 minutes, using the stir button occasionally, until beginning to brown a little. Add the potato and spinach, cover and cook for 3–4 minutes, using the stir button occasionally, until beginning to steam.

3 Add the remaining ingredients except the salmon and haddock pieces. Cover, stir to mix and bring just up to the boil. Immediately reduce the heat to simmer and cook for the remaining time using the stir button occasionally.
10–15 minutes before the end of the cooking time stir the salmon and haddock pieces into the soup and simmer until cooked through. Blend to the consistency you prefer. Season to taste, if necessary.

4 Ladle or pour the piping hot soup into bowls. Serve immediately with hot crusty bread.

JUG-STYLE SOUP MAKER

Remove any bones from the salmon and haddock. Cut into bite-sized pieces and poach in a little stock until cooked. Put all the prepared ingredients except the pieces of salmon and smoked haddock (step 1 above) and other ingredients into the metal jug. Secure the lid in place. Select the chunky function and leave to cook. 6–8 minutes before the end of the cooking time stir the salmon and smoked haddock pieces into the soup, cover and continue cooking. Season to taste, if necessary. Serve the soup as in step 4 above.

Fishy Tomato and Cavolo Nero Soup with Green Olives

This is a serious soup, packed with flavour.

SERVES 4
1 onion
2 garlic cloves
200g (7oz) sweet potato
1 lemon
4 large cavolo nero leaves
400g (14oz) mixed skinless fish pieces such as salmon,
    mackerel, whiting, haddock or trout
1 tbsp olive oil
400ml (14fl oz) fish, vegetable or chicken stock
400ml (14fl oz) passata
2 tbsp lemon juice
Freshly milled black pepper, to taste
A few pitted, sliced green olives and olive oil, to serve

1   Finely chop the onion and garlic. Chop the sweet potato into
    small pieces. Cut the lemon in half and squeeze out the juice.
    Cut the stiff ribs from the cavolo nero and thinly slice the frilly
    leaves. Remove any bones from the fish pieces and cut into bite-
    sized portions.
2   Put the oil into the glass jar. Set the timer to 25 minutes and the
    temperature to high. Add the onion and garlic, cover and cook
    for 1–2 minutes, using the stir button occasionally, until
    beginning to brown a little. Add the cavolo nero and sweet
    potato, cover and cook for 3–4 minutes, using the stir button
    occasionally, until beginning to steam.

3   Add the remaining ingredients except the fish pieces. Cover, stir to
    mix and bring just up to the boil. Immediately reduce the heat to
    simmer and cook for the remaining time using the stir button
    occasionally. 10–15 minutes before the end of the cooking time stir
    the fish pieces into the soup and simmer until cooked through.
    Blend to the consistency you prefer. Season to taste, if necessary.
4   Ladle or pour the piping hot soup into bowls. Drizzle over a little
    oil, top with a few olive slices and serve immediately.

JUG-STYLE SOUP MAKER
Remove any bones from the fish. Cut into bite-sized pieces and
poach in a little stock until cooked. Put all the prepared ingredients
except the fish pieces (step 1 above) and other ingredients into the
metal jug. Secure the lid in place. Select the chunky function and
leave to cook. 6–8 minutes before the end of the cooking time stir the
fish pieces into the soup, cover and continue cooking. Season to
taste, if necessary. Serve the soup as in step 4 above.

Pan-Fried Tuna in a Fish Broth

Tuna is a very 'meaty' fish. It's a lovely way to serve it in a bowl with the fish broth poured over.

SERVES 4
1 onion
2 garlic cloves
2 spring onions
1 celery stick
2 courgettes
1 lime
2.5cm (1in) piece of root ginger
3 large handfuls of sea vegetables
3 large handfuls of spinach leaves
1 tbsp olive oil, plus extra
700ml (1¼ pints) fish, vegetable or chicken stock
Freshly milled black pepper, to taste
4 tuna steaks

1   Finely chop the onion and garlic. Roughly slice the spring onions. Finely chop the celery and the courgettes. Cut the lime in half and squeeze out the juice. Grate the ginger. Shred the spinach leaves and sea vegetables.
2   Put the oil into the glass jar. Set the timer to 20 minutes and the temperature to high. Add the onion, garlic and spring onions, cover and cook for 1–2 minutes, using the stir button occasionally, until beginning to brown a little. Add the celery and courgettes, cover and cook for 4–5 minutes, using the stir button occasionally, until beginning to steam.
3   Add the remaining ingredients except the tuna steaks. Cover, stir to mix and bring just up to the boil. Immediately reduce the heat to simmer and cook for the remaining time, using the stir button occasionally. Blend to the consistency you prefer. Season to taste, if necessary.

4   While the soup is cooking, heat a little oil in a frying pan and cook the tuna steaks on both sides until cooked to your liking.
5   Put the hot tuna steaks into bowls and ladle or pour the piping hot soup over. Serve immediately.

JUG-STYLE SOUP MAKER

Put all the prepared ingredients (step 1 above) and other ingredients except the tuna steaks into the metal jug. Secure the lid in place. Select the chunky function and leave to cook. While the soup is cooking, cook the tuna steaks (step 4 above). Season the soup to taste, if necessary. Serve the soup as in step 5 above.

Salmon, Edamame and Courgette Soup

Five-spice powder is made up of various ground spices, such as star anise, cinnamon, fennel seeds, ginger and pepper.

SERVES 4
1 onion
2 celery sticks
2 courgettes
400g (14oz) skinless salmon fillet
1 tbsp olive oil
700ml (1¼ pints) fish, vegetable or chicken stock
250g (9oz) edamame beans, fresh or frozen
2 tsp five-spice powder
Freshly milled black pepper, to taste
Two chopped anchovy fillets mixed with 3 tbsp toasted seeds, to serve

1 Finely chop the onion, celery sticks and the courgettes. Remove any bones from the salmon fillet and cut into bite-sized pieces.
2 Put the oil into the glass jar. Set the timer to 30 minutes and the temperature to high. Add the onion, cover and cook for 1–2 minutes, using the stir button occasionally, until beginning to soften. Add the celery and courgettes, cover and cook for 4–5 minutes, using the stir button occasionally, until beginning to steam.

3 Add the remaining ingredients except the salmon pieces. Cover, stir to mix and bring just up to the boil. Immediately reduce the heat to simmer and cook for the remaining time, using the stir button occasionally. 10–15 minutes before the end of the cooking time stir the salmon pieces into the soup and simmer until cooked through. Blend to the consistency you prefer. Season to taste, if necessary.
4 Ladle or pour the piping hot soup into bowls and serve immediately with the anchovy and seed mix on the side.

JUG-STYLE SOUP MAKER

Remove any bones from the salmon fillet. Cut into bite-sized pieces and poach in a little stock until cooked. Put all the prepared ingredients except the salmon pieces (step 1 above) and other ingredients into the metal jug. Secure the lid in place. Select the chunky function and leave to cook. 6–8 minutes before the end of the cooking time stir the salmon pieces into the soup, cover and continue cooking. Season to taste, if necessary. Serve the soup as in step 4 above.

Sea Fish, Mushroom and Broccoli Soup with Squid Ink Pasta

The black, squid-ink pasta makes this soup look very dramatic, but you can use plain spaghetti if you don't have any.

SERVES 4

1 red onion

1 small fennel bulb

200g (7oz) broccoli florets

250g (9oz) chestnut button mushrooms

400g (14oz) mixed skinless fish such as salmon, whiting, haddock or trout

2 tbsp olive oil

700ml (1¼ pints) fish or vegetable stock

1 tsp tomato purée

1 tbsp lemon juice

Freshly milled black pepper, to taste

300g (10½oz) squid ink spaghetti

Chopped fennel leaves, to serve

1   Finely chop the onion and thinly slice the fennel bulb. If large, cut the broccoli florets into smaller pieces. Quarter the mushrooms. Remove any bones from the fish and cut into bite-sized pieces.

2   Put the oil into the glass jar. Set the timer to 30 minutes and the temperature to high. Add the onion, cover and cook for 1–2 minutes, using the stir button occasionally, until beginning to brown a little. Add the fennel and broccoli, cover and cook for 4–5 minutes, using the stir button occasionally, until beginning to steam.

3   Add the remaining ingredients except the fish pieces and
    spaghetti. Cover, stir to mix and bring just up to the boil.
    Immediately reduce the heat to simmer and cook for the
    remaining time, using the stir button occasionally. 10–15
    minutes before the end of the cooking time stir the fish pieces
    into the soup and simmer until cooked through. While the soup
    is cooking, cook the spaghetti following the packet instructions.
    Blend the soup to the consistency you prefer. Season to taste, if
    necessary.
4   Pile the hot spaghetti into bowls and ladle or pour the piping hot
    soup over. Sprinkle over a little chopped fennel leaves and serve
    immediately.

JUG-STYLE SOUP MAKER

Remove any bones from the fish. Cut into bite-sized pieces and
poach in a little stock until cooked. Put all the prepared ingredients
except the fish pieces (step 1 above) and other ingredients into the
metal jug. Secure the lid in place. Select the chunky function and
leave to cook. 6–8 minutes before the end of the cooking time stir the
fish pieces into the soup, cover and continue cooking. While the soup
is cooking, cook the pasta following the packet instructions. Season
the soup to taste, if necessary. Serve the soup as in step 4 above.

Fish, Pepper and Couscous Soup

Tamarind paste adds a sweet-sour flavour with a hint of lemon and dates.

SERVES 4
1 leek
1 red pepper
½ a small iceberg lettuce
350g (12oz) mixed skinless fish such as herring, salmon, mackerel or trout
1 tbsp olive oil
400ml (14fl oz) fish or vegetable stock
200ml (7fl oz) vegetable or chicken stock
400g can chopped tomatoes
2 tsp tamarind paste
Freshly milled black pepper, to taste
100g (3½oz) large couscous

1 Finely chop the leek. Cut the red pepper in half, remove the stalk and seeds and finely chop. Separate out the lettuce leaves and thinly slice. Remove any bones from the fish and cut into bite-sized pieces.
2 Put the oil into the glass jar. Set the timer to 25 minutes and the temperature to high. Add the leek, cover and cook for 3–4 minutes, using the stir button occasionally, until beginning to soften. Add the pepper, cover and cook for 1–2 minutes, using the stir button occasionally, until beginning to steam.
3 Add the remaining ingredients except the fish pieces and couscous. Cover, stir to mix and bring just up to the boil. Immediately reduce the heat to simmer and cook for the remaining time, using the stir button occasionally. 10–15 minutes before the end of the cooking time stir the fish pieces into the soup and simmer until cooked through.

4 While the soup is cooking, cook the couscous following the packet instructions. Blend the soup leaving it chunky. Stir the hot couscous into the soup. Season to taste, if necessary.

5 Ladle or pour the piping hot soup into bowls and serve immediately.

JUG-STYLE SOUP MAKER

Remove any bones from the fish. Cut into bite-sized pieces and poach in a little stock until cooked. Put all the prepared ingredients except the fish pieces (step 1 above) and other ingredients except the couscous into the metal jug. Secure the lid in place. Select the chunky function and leave to cook. 6–8 minutes before the end of the cooking time stir the fish pieces into the soup, cover and continue cooking. While the soup is cooking, follow step 4 above to cook the couscous and stir into the soup. Season to taste, if necessary. Serve the soup as in step 5 above.

Monkfish, Shrimp and Sorrel Soup

Monkfish is a very firm fish. It's widely available, but you could use tuna or salmon as an alternative if you need to.

SERVES 4
1 onion
2 large handfuls of sorrel leaves
2 large handfuls of spinach leaves
175g (6oz) long round beans
2.5cm (1in) piece of root ginger
350g (12oz) monkfish
1 tbsp olive oil
700ml (1¼ pints) fish, vegetable or chicken stock
Freshly milled black pepper, to taste
140g (5oz) cooked, shelled shrimps
Lemon wedges, to serve.

1   Finely chop the onion. Thinly slice the sorrel and spinach. Cut the long beans into chunks. Grate the root ginger. Cut the monkfish into bite-sized pieces.
2   Put the oil into the glass jar. Set the timer to 20 minutes and the temperature to high. Add the onion, cover and cook for 1–2 minutes, using the stir button occasionally, until beginning to brown a little. Add the beans, cover and cook for 2–3 minutes, using the stir button occasionally, until beginning to steam.
3   Add the remaining ingredients except the monkfish pieces and shrimps. Cover, stir to mix and bring just up to the boil. Immediately reduce the heat to simmer and cook for the remaining time, using the stir button occasionally. 10–15 minutes before the end of the cooking time stir the monkfish pieces into the soup and simmer until cooked through. Add the shrimps for the last 2 minutes to heat through. Blend but leave chunky. Season to taste, if necessary.

4 Ladle or pour the piping hot soup into bowls. Serve immediately with lemon wedges to squeeze over.

JUG-STYLE SOUP MAKER

Cut the monkfish into bite-sized pieces and poach in a little stock until cooked. Put all the prepared ingredients except the monkfish pieces (step 1 above) and other ingredients except the shrimps into the metal jug. Secure the lid in place. Select the chunky function and leave to cook. 6–8 minutes before the end of the cooking time stir the monkfish pieces and shrimps into the soup, cover and continue cooking. Season to taste, if necessary. Serve the soup as in step 4 above.

Fragrant Green Herb and Fish Soup

This soup seems a bit special – it's perfect to share with your friends.

SERVES 4
2 shallots
2 red peppers
2 lemongrass stalks
Large handful of rocket leaves
Large handful of coriander leaves
Large handful of basil leaves
2 large handfuls of spinach leaves
400g (14oz) mixed skinless fish such as salmon, cod,
    haddock or trout
1 tbsp olive oil
700ml (1¼ pints) fish, vegetable or chicken stock
Pinch of ground turmeric
Freshly milled black pepper, to taste

1   Finely chop the shallots. Cut the red peppers in half. Remove
    the stalks and seeds and finely chop. Pull the tough outer leaves
    off the lemongrass stalks and finely chop the remainder. Thinly
    slice the rocket, coriander, basil and spinach leaves. Remove any
    bones from the fish and cut into bite-sized pieces.
2   Put the oil into the glass jar. Set the timer to 20 minutes and the
    temperature to high. Add the shallots, cover and cook for 1–2
    minutes, using the stir button occasionally, until beginning to
    soften. Add the peppers, cover and cook for 2–3 minutes, using
    the stir button occasionally, until beginning to steam.

3   Add the remaining ingredients except the fish pieces. Cover, stir
    to mix and bring just up to the boil. Immediately reduce the heat
    to simmer and cook for the remaining time, using the stir button
    occasionally. 10–15 minutes before the end of the cooking time
    stir the fish pieces into the soup and simmer until cooked
    through. Blend to the consistency you prefer. Season to taste, if
    necessary.
4   Ladle or pour the piping hot soup into bowls. Serve
    immediately.

JUG-STYLE SOUP MAKER

Remove any bones from the fish. Cut into bite-sized pieces and
poach in a little stock until cooked. Put all the prepared ingredients
except the fish pieces (step 1 above) and other ingredients into the
metal jug. Secure the lid in place. Select the chunky function and
leave to cook. 6–8 minutes before the end of the cooking time stir the
salmon pieces into the soup, cover and continue cooking. Season to
taste, if necessary. Serve the soup as in step 4 above.

Poultry, Game and Meat

Meat is a rich source of protein, so all these poultry, game and meat recipes are really healthy and nutritious. Even more so, because each soup contains a matching partner or two from the superfood repertoire. And there are some mouth-watering soups here to savour – enticing variations on chicken, beef and turkey; substantial soups with pasta (duck with tagliatelle and chilli pork with spaghetti); and lovely lean-meat soups with venison and gammon and beans. Remember to always cook the meat before using it in a jug-style soup maker.

Ginger Chicken and Lemongrass Soup

When using lemongrass in an electric soup maker only use the soft inner leaves, as the outer leaves are woody.

SERVES 4
1 onion
2 celery sticks
2 carrots
2.5cm (1in) piece of root ginger
Large bunch of coriander leaves
2 lemongrass stalks
350g (12oz) skinless boneless chicken
2 tbsp olive oil
700ml (1¼ pints) poultry or game stock
Freshly milled black pepper, to taste
Coriander leaves, to serve

1   Finely chop the onion. Thinly slice the celery sticks. Finely chop the carrots. Finely grate the root ginger. Pull the coriander leaves from the stalks. Pull the tough outer leaves off the lemongrass stalks and finely chop the remainder. Cut the chicken into small pieces.
2   Put the oil into the glass jar. Set the timer to 30 minutes and the temperature to simmer. Add the chicken and onion, cover and cook for 12–15 minutes until the chicken is cooked through, using the stir button occasionally.
3   Increase the heat to high. Add the celery and carrots and cook for 2–4 minutes until steaming.

4   Add the remaining ingredients. Cover, stir to mix and bring to
    the boil for 2 minutes. Reduce the heat to simmer and cook for
    the remaining time, using the stir button occasionally. Blend to
    the consistency you prefer. Season to taste, if necessary.
5   Ladle or pour the piping hot soup into bowls. Top with
    coriander leaves and serve immediately.

JUG-STYLE SOUP MAKER

Cut the chicken into small pieces and poach in a little stock until
cooked. Put all the prepared ingredients (step 1 above) and other
ingredients into the metal jug. Secure the lid in place. Select the
chunky function and leave to cook. Season to taste, if necessary.
Serve the soup as in step 5 above.

Beef and Squash Soup with Grains

Horseradish and beef are a perfect pairing, but if it's too hot for your taste use milder wholegrain mustard.

SERVES 4

1 red onion

2 courgettes

300g (10½oz) wedge of butternut squash

300g (10½oz) lean beefsteak

1 tbsp olive oil

700ml (1¼ pints) meat stock

Freshly milled black pepper, to taste

1–2 tsp horseradish sauce

250g sachet of ready-to-eat mixed grains such as quinoa grains and red rice

1   Finely chop the onion. Cut the courgettes into small pieces. Remove any seeds from the butternut squash, peel and cut into small cubes. Cut the beef into small pieces.

2   Put the oil into the glass jar. Set the timer to 30 minutes and the temperature to simmer. Add the beef pieces, cover and cook for 15 minutes, using the stir button occasionally.

3   Increase the heat to high. Add the onion, courgettes and butternut squash, cook for 3–5 minutes until steaming.

4   Add the remaining ingredients except the grains. Cover, stir to mix and bring to the boil for 2 minutes. Reduce the heat to simmer and cook for the remaining time, using the stir button occasionally. Check on the beef – if it's not tender add another 10–15 minutes to the cooking cycle.

5 While the soup is cooking, heat the grains following the packet instructions. Blend the soup to the consistency you prefer. Season to taste, if necessary.

6 Spoon the hot grains into bowls. Ladle or pour over the piping hot soup. Serve immediately.

JUG-STYLE SOUP MAKER

Cut the beef into small pieces and cook in a little stock. Put all the prepared ingredients (step 1 above) and other ingredients except the grains into the metal jug. Secure the lid in place. Select the chunky function and leave to cook. Meanwhile heat the grains (see step 5 above). Blend the soup to the consistency you prefer. Season to taste, if necessary. Serve the soup as in step 6 above.

Game Soup

Packs of mixed, diced game are available from many butchers and supermarkets.

SERVES 4
1 onion
2 carrots
6 large curly kale leaves
2 sprigs of thyme
8 cooked chestnuts, frozen or vacuum-packed
2 juniper berries
350g (12oz) boneless game meat such as pheasant,
    venison or rabbit
1 tbsp olive oil
700ml (1¼ pints) game or meat stock
Freshly milled black pepper, to taste
Thyme leaves, to serve

1   Finely chop the onion. Thinly slice the carrots. Cut and discard
    the stiff ribs from the curly kale leaves and thinly slice. Pull the
    thyme leaves from the stalks. Roughly chop the chestnuts.
    Crush the juniper berries. Cut the meat into small pieces.
2   Put the oil into the glass jar. Set the timer to 30 minutes and the
    temperature to simmer. Add the meat pieces, cover and cook for
    15 minutes, using the stir button occasionally.
3   Increase the heat to high. Add the onion, carrots and curly kale
    and cook for 3–5 minutes until steaming.

4   Add the remaining ingredients. Cover, stir to mix and bring to the boil for 2 minutes. Reduce the heat to simmer and cook for the remaining time, using the stir button occasionally. Check on the meat – if it's not tender add another 10–15 minutes to the cooking cycle. Blend to the consistency you prefer. Season to taste, if necessary.
5   Ladle or pour the piping hot soup into bowls. Scatter over a few thyme leaves and serve immediately.

JUG-STYLE SOUP MAKER

Cut the game meat into small pieces and cook in a little stock. Put all the prepared ingredients (step 1 above) and other ingredients into the metal jug. Secure the lid in place. Select the chunky function and leave to cook. Blend to the consistency you prefer. Season to taste, if necessary. Serve the soup as in step 5 above.

Turkey, Sage and Chestnut Soup

Enjoy all the flavours of a festive dinner, in a bowl. This is a great way to use up leftover turkey.

SERVES 4
1 onion
1 garlic clove
1 celery stick
1 carrot
Large handful of small chard leaves
8 cooked chestnuts, frozen or vacuum-packed
4 sage leaves
350g (12oz) skinless boneless turkey
2 tbsp olive oil
700ml (1¼ pints) poultry or game stock
Freshly milled black pepper, to taste
Hot baguettes, to serve

1 Finely chop the onion and garlic. Thinly slice the celery stick. Finely chop the carrot. Slice the chard leaves. Roughly chop the chestnuts. Tear the sage leaves in half. Cut the turkey into small pieces.

2 Put the oil into the glass jar. Set the timer to 30 minutes and the temperature to simmer. Add the turkey, cover and cook for 12–15 minutes until the turkey is cooked through using the stir button occasionally. If you're using cooked turkey, miss out this stage and add the turkey in step 4.

3 Increase the heat to high. Add the onion, garlic and carrot and cook for 2–4 minutes, until steaming.

4 Add the remaining ingredients. Cover, stir to mix and bring to the boil for 2 minutes. Reduce the heat to simmer and cook for the remaining time, using the stir button occasionally. Blend to the consistency you prefer. Season to taste, if necessary.
5 Ladle or pour the piping hot soup into bowls. Serve immediately with hot baguettes.

JUG-STYLE SOUP MAKER

Cut the turkey into small pieces and poach in a little stock until cooked. Thaw the chestnuts before you start if they are frozen. Put all the prepared ingredients (step 1 above) and other ingredients into the metal jug. Secure the lid in place. Select the chunky function and leave to cook. Season to taste, if necessary. Serve the soup as in step 5 above.

Venison Soup

Guinea fowl or corn-fed chicken would also work well if you can't find venison.

SERVES 4

3 shallots
2 carrots
1 small sweet potato, about 200g (7oz)
300g (10½oz) red cabbage
Small bunch of parsley
350g (12oz) boneless venison
1 tbsp olive oil
600ml (1 pint) game or meat stock
150ml (¼ pint) passata
Freshly milled black pepper, to taste
8 cranberries, fresh or frozen
Hot crusty bread, to serve

1   Finely chop the shallots. Thinly slice the carrots. Cut the sweet potato into small pieces. Thinly slice the red cabbage. Pull the parsley leaves from the stalks and finely chop. Cut the venison into small pieces.
2   Put the oil into the glass jar. Set the timer to 30 minutes and the temperature to simmer. Add the venison pieces, cover and cook for 15 minutes using the stir button occasionally.
3   Increase the heat to high. Add the shallots, carrots and sweet potato and cook for 3–5 minutes until steaming.

4   Add the remaining ingredients. Cover, stir to mix and bring to the boil for 2 minutes. Reduce the heat to simmer and cook for the remaining time using the stir button occasionally. Check on the venison – if it's not tender add another 10–15 minutes to the cooking cycle. Blend to the consistency you prefer. Season to taste, if necessary.
5   Ladle or pour the piping hot soup into bowls. Serve immediately with hot crusty bread.

JUG-STYLE SOUP MAKER

Cut the venison into small pieces and cook in a little stock. Put all the prepared ingredients (step 1 above) and other ingredients into the metal jug. Secure the lid in place. Select the chunky function and leave to cook. Blend to the consistency you prefer. Season to taste, if necessary. Serve the soup as in step 5 above.

Chicken, Bean and Pea Soup

Use good quality chicken for the best flavour.

SERVES 4
2 shallots
1 celery stick
1 carrot
140g (5oz) runner beans
200g can borlotti beans
300g (10½oz) skinless boneless chicken
2 tbsp olive oil
700ml (1¼ pints) poultry or game stock
Freshly milled black pepper, to taste
150g (5½oz) peas, fresh or frozen
2 tbsp wholegrain mustard
Hot baguettes, to serve

1 Finely chop the shallots. Thinly slice the celery stick. Finely chop the carrot. Top and tail the runner beans removing any strings. Drain the can of beans. Cut the chicken into small pieces.
2 Put the oil into the glass jar. Set the timer to 30 minutes and the temperature to simmer. Add the chicken and shallots, cover and cook for 12–15 minutes until the chicken is cooked through, using the stir button occasionally.
3 Increase the heat to high. Add the carrot and cook for 2–4 minutes until steaming.
4 Add the remaining ingredients. Cover, stir to mix and bring to the boil for 2 minutes. Reduce the heat to simmer and cook for the remaining time, using the stir button occasionally. Blend to the consistency you prefer. Season to taste, if necessary.

5 Ladle or pour the piping hot soup into bowls. Serve immediately with hot baguettes.

JUG-STYLE SOUP MAKER
Cut the chicken into small pieces and poach in a little stock until cooked. Thaw the peas before you start if they are frozen. Put all the prepared ingredients (step 1 above) and other ingredients into the metal jug. Secure the lid in place. Select the chunky function and leave to cook. Season to taste, if necessary. Serve the soup as in step 5 above.

Spicy Beef and Onion Soup

This soup has all the flavours of traditional Hungarian goulash with lots of paprika and cayenne pepper.

SERVES 4
1 Spanish onion
2 garlic cloves
1 red pepper
400g (14oz) cauliflower florets
300g (10½oz) lean beefsteak
1 tbsp olive oil
600ml (1 pint) meat stock
150ml (¼ pint) passata
1 tbsp tomato purée
2 tbsp sweet paprika pepper
1 tsp hot cayenne pepper
1 tsp caraway seeds
Freshly milled black pepper, to taste
Natural yogurt or single cream and chopped parsley, to serve

1   Finely chop the onion and garlic. Cut the pepper in half, remove the stalk and seeds and thinly slice. Cut the cauliflower florets into small pieces. Cut the beef into small pieces.
2   Put the oil into the glass jar. Set the timer to 30 minutes and the temperature to simmer. Add the beef pieces, cover and cook for 15 minutes, using the stir button occasionally.
3   Increase the heat to high. Add the onion, garlic and cauliflower, cook for 3–5 minutes until steaming.

4 Add the remaining ingredients. Cover, stir to mix and bring to the boil for 2 minutes. Reduce the heat to simmer and cook for the remaining time, using the stir button occasionally. Check on the beef – if it's not tender add another 10–15 minutes to the cooking cycle. Blend to the consistency you prefer. Season to taste, if necessary.

5 Ladle or pour the piping hot soup into bowls. Top with a swirl of yogurt or cream and chopped parsley. Serve immediately.

JUG-STYLE SOUP MAKER

Cut the beef into small pieces and cook in a little stock. Put all the prepared ingredients (step 1 above) and other ingredients into the metal jug. Secure the lid in place. Select the chunky function and leave to cook. Blend to the consistency you prefer. Season to taste, if necessary. Serve the soup as in step 5 above.

Chicken, Fennel and Sesame Seed Soup

Fennel gives a background aniseed flavour to the soup.

SERVES 4
6 spring onions
1 carrot
1 fennel bulb
1 pak choi
2 large handfuls of small spinach leaves
1 tbsp cornflour
300g (10½oz) skinless boneless chicken
2 tbsp olive oil
700ml (1¼ pints) poultry or game stock
Freshly milled black pepper, to taste
2 tbsp low-salt soy sauce
Large handful of bean sprouts
2 tbsp toasted sesame seeds
Chopped toasted cashew nuts, to serve

1 Thinly slice the spring onions. Finely chop the carrot and the fennel bulb. Thinly slice the pak choi. Roughly slice the spinach leaves. In a cup, mix the cornflour to a smooth paste with a little cold water. Cut the chicken into small pieces.

2 Put the oil into the glass jar. Set the timer to 30 minutes and the temperature to simmer. Add the chicken and spring onions, cover and cook for 12–15 minutes, until the chicken is cooked through, using the stir button occasionally.

3 Increase the heat to high. Add the carrot and pak choi and cook for 2–4 minutes, until steaming.

4 Add the remaining ingredients except the bean sprouts and sesame seeds. Cover, stir to mix and bring to the boil for 2 minutes. Reduce the heat to simmer and cook for the remaining time, using the stir button occasionally. 2–3 minutes before the end of the cooking time stir the bean sprouts and sesame seeds into the soup. Blend to the consistency you prefer. Season to taste, if necessary.

5 Ladle or pour the piping hot soup into bowls. Sprinkle over a few chopped cashew nuts and serve immediately.

JUG-STYLE SOUP MAKER

Cut the chicken into small pieces and poach in a little stock until cooked. Put all the prepared ingredients (step 1 above) and other ingredients except the bean sprouts and sesame seeds into the metal jug. Secure the lid in place. Select the chunky function and leave to cook. 2–3 minutes before the end of the cooking time stir the bean sprouts and sesame seeds into the soup. Season to taste, if necessary. Serve the soup as in step 5 above.

Gammon and Bean Soup

For a stronger flavour, try using smoked gammon.

SERVES 4
1 onion
1 celery stick
1 carrot
350g (12oz) lean unsmoked gammon
1 tbsp olive oil
700ml (1¼ pints) meat or chicken stock
200g (7oz) broad beans, fresh or frozen
200g (7oz) edamame beans, fresh or frozen
½ tsp dried mixed herbs
Freshly milled black pepper, to taste
Celery leaves and grated cheese, to serve

1 Finely chop the onion. Thinly slice the celery. Finely chop the carrot. Cut the gammon into small pieces.
2 Put the oil into the glass jar. Set the timer to 30 minutes and the temperature to simmer. Add the gammon pieces, cover and cook for 15 minutes, using the stir button occasionally.
3 Increase the heat to high. Add the onion, celery and carrot, cook for 3–5 minutes, until steaming.
4 Add the remaining ingredients. Cover, stir to mix and bring to the boil for 2 minutes. Reduce the heat to simmer and cook for the remaining time, using the stir button occasionally. Check on the gammon – if it's not tender add another 10–15 minutes to the cooking cycle.

5 Blend the soup to the consistency you prefer. Season to taste, if necessary.

6 Ladle or pour the piping hot soup into bowls. Top with a celery leaf and serve immediately with grated cheese to sprinkle over.

JUG-STYLE SOUP MAKER

Cut the gammon into small pieces and cook in a little stock. Put all the prepared ingredients (step 1 above) and other ingredients into the metal jug. Secure the lid in place. Select the chunky function and leave to cook. Blend the soup to the consistency you prefer. Season to taste, if necessary. Serve the soup as in step 6 above.

Turkey Coconut Curry Soup

This soup has the light, fresh flavours of a Thai curry.

SERVES 4
6 spring onions
2 garlic cloves
2 lemongrass stalks
1 lime
Large handful of spinach leaves
250g (9oz) broccoli florets
350g (12oz) skinless boneless turkey
2 tbsp olive oil
600ml (1 pint) poultry or game stock
200ml (7fl oz) coconut milk
2 tbsp Thai green curry paste
Large handful of basil leaves
Freshly milled black pepper, to taste
Hot naan breads, to serve

1   Thinly slice the spring onions. Crush the garlic. Pull the tough outer leaves off the lemongrass stalks and finely chop the remainder. Cut the lime in half and squeeze out the juice. Shred the spinach leaves. Cut the broccoli florets into small pieces. Cut the turkey into small pieces.
2   Put the oil into the glass jar. Set the timer to 30 minutes and the temperature to simmer. Add the turkey, cover and cook for 12–15 minutes until the turkey is cooked through, using the stir button occasionally.
3   Increase the heat to high. Add the spring onions, garlic and broccoli and cook for 2–4 minutes, until steaming.

4 Add the remaining ingredients. Cover, stir to mix and bring to the boil for 2 minutes. Reduce the heat to simmer and cook for the remaining time, using the stir button occasionally. Blend to the consistency you prefer. Season to taste, if necessary.

5 Ladle or pour the piping hot soup into bowls. Serve immediately with hot naan breads.

JUG-STYLE SOUP MAKER

Cut the turkey into small pieces and poach in a little stock until cooked. Put all the prepared ingredients (step 1 above) and other ingredients into the metal jug. Secure the lid in place. Select the chunky function and leave to cook. Season to taste, if necessary. Serve the soup as in step 5 above.

Duck Soup with Tagliatelle

Fruit and duck are a perfect combination.

SERVES 4
1 onion
200g (7oz) savoy cabbage
200g (7oz) red cabbage
1 eating apple
1 small orange
2 skinless duck breasts
1 tbsp olive oil
700ml (1¼ pints) poultry or game stock
Freshly milled black pepper, to taste
2 tsp five-spice powder
140g (5oz) fresh tagliatelle
Chopped parsley, to serve

1 Finely chop the onion. Shred the savoy cabbage and red cabbage. Peel, core and finely chop the apple. Finely zest the rind from half the orange, cut in half and squeeze out all the juice. Cut the duck breasts into small pieces.
2 Put the oil into the glass jar. Set the timer to 30 minutes and the temperature to simmer. Add the duck pieces, cover and cook for 12–15 minutes until the duck is cooked through, using the stir button occasionally.
3 Increase the heat to high. Add the onion, savoy and red cabbage and cook for 3–5 minutes, until steaming.
4 Add the remaining ingredients except the tagliatelle. Cover, stir to mix and bring to the boil for 2 minutes. Reduce the heat to simmer and cook for the remaining time, using the stir button occasionally. Blend to the consistency you prefer. Season to taste, if necessary.

5 While the soup is cooking, cook the tagliatelle following the packet instructions.

6 Spoon the piping hot tagliatelle into bowls and ladle or pour the steaming hot soup over. Scatter over a little chopped parsley and serve.

JUG-STYLE SOUP MAKER
Cut the duck breasts into small pieces and cook in a little stock. Put all the prepared ingredients (step 1 above) and other ingredients except the tagliatelle into the metal jug. Secure the lid in place. Select the chunky function and leave to cook. To cook the tagliatelle follow step 5 above. Season the soup to taste, if necessary. Serve the soup as in step 6 above.

Chicken, Mushroom and Thyme Soup

Swiss chard works well in this soup in place of the Chinese leaves.

SERVES 4
1 onion
1 small leek
2 celery sticks
2 carrots
200g (7oz) Chinese leaves
250g (9oz) mushrooms
2 sprigs of thyme
350g (12oz) skinless boneless chicken
1 tbsp olive oil
700ml (1¼ pints) poultry, game or mushroom stock
Freshly milled black pepper, to taste

1 Finely chop the onion. Thinly slice the leek and celery sticks. Finely chop the carrots. Shred the Chinese leaves. Thinly slice the mushrooms. Pull the thyme leaves from stalks. Cut the chicken into small pieces.
2 Put the oil into the glass jar. Set the timer to 30 minutes and the temperature to simmer. Add the chicken pieces, cover and cook for 12–15 minutes, until the chicken is cooked through, using the stir button occasionally.
3 Increase the heat to high. Add the onion, leek and celery and cook for 3–5 minutes, until steaming.

4   Add the remaining ingredients. Cover, stir to mix and bring to the boil for 2 minutes. Reduce the heat to simmer and cook for the remaining time using the stir button occasionally. Blend to the consistency you prefer. Season to taste, if necessary.
5   Ladle or pour the piping hot soup into bowls. Serve immediately.

JUG-STYLE SOUP MAKER
Cut the chicken into small pieces and poach in a little stock until cooked. Put all the prepared ingredients (step 1 above) and other ingredients into the metal jug. Secure the lid in place. Select the chunky function and leave to cook. Blend to the consistency you prefer. Season to taste, if necessary. Serve the soup as in step 5 above.

Lamb and Rosemary Soup with Grains

Only use a few rosemary leaves, as the flavour can be very dominant.

SERVES 4
1 red onion
2 small carrots, or one if large
250g (9oz) purple sprouting broccoli
Large handful of small spinach leaves
6–8 rosemary leaves
350g (12oz) lean lamb
1 tbsp olive oil
700ml (1¼ pints) meat stock
Freshly milled black pepper, to taste
250g sachet of ready-to-eat mixed grains such as barley, wheatberries, spelt and rice

1   Finely chop the onion. Thinly slice the carrots. Cut the purple sprouting broccoli into small pieces. Roughly slice the spinach leaves. Finely chop the rosemary leaves. Cut the lamb into small pieces.
2   Put the oil into the glass jar. Set the timer to 30 minutes and the temperature to simmer. Add the lamb pieces, cover and cook for 15 minutes, using the stir button occasionally.
3   Increase the heat to high. Add the onion, carrots and purple sprouting broccoli, cook for 3–5 minutes, until steaming.
4   Add the remaining ingredients except the grains. Cover, stir to mix and bring to the boil for 2 minutes. Reduce the heat to simmer and cook for the remaining time, using the stir button occasionally. Check on the lamb – if it's not tender add another 10–15 minutes to the cooking cycle.

5 While the soup is cooking, heat the grains following the packet instructions. Blend the soup to the consistency you prefer. Season to taste, if necessary

6 Spoon the hot grains into bowls. Ladle or pour over the piping hot soup. Serve immediately.

JUG-STYLE SOUP MAKER

Cut the lamb into small pieces and cook in a little stock. Put all the prepared ingredients (step 1 above) and other ingredients except the grains into the metal jug. Secure the lid in place. Select the chunky function and leave to cook. Meanwhile heat the grains (see step 5 above). Blend the soup to the consistency you prefer. Season to taste, if necessary. Serve the soup as in step 6 above.

Chilli Pork Soup with Spaghetti

Hoisin sauce adds an Asian flavour to this soup.

SERVES 4
6 spring onions
2 pak choi
Large handful of small spinach leaves
250g (9oz) Chinese leaves
1 eating apple
350g (12oz) lean pork
1 tbsp olive oil
700ml (1¼ pints) meat or chicken stock
Freshly milled black pepper, to taste
3 tbsp hoisin sauce
2–3 tsp chilli paste
300g (10½oz) fresh spaghetti
Grated Parmesan or pecorino cheese, to serve

1   Finely chop the spring onions. Thinly slice the pak choi, spinach leaves and Chinese leaves. Peel, core and finely chop the apple. Cut the pork into small pieces.
2   Put the oil into the glass jar. Set the timer to 30 minutes and the temperature to simmer. Add the pork pieces, cover and cook for 15 minutes, using the stir button occasionally.
3   Increase the heat to high. Add the spring onions, pak choi, spinach leaves and Chinese leaves, cook for 3–5 minutes until steaming.
4   Add the remaining ingredients except the spaghetti. Cover, stir to mix and bring to the boil for 2 minutes. Reduce the heat to simmer and cook for the remaining time, using the stir button occasionally. Check on the pork – if it's not tender add another 10–15 minutes to the cooking cycle.

5 While the soup is cooking, cook the spaghetti following the packet instructions. Blend the soup to the consistency you prefer. Season to taste, if necessary.

6 Spoon the hot spaghetti into bowls. Ladle or pour over the piping hot soup. Serve immediately with grated cheese to sprinkle over.

JUG-STYLE SOUP MAKER

Cut the pork into small pieces and cook in a little stock. Put all the prepared ingredients (step 1 above) and other ingredients except the spaghetti into the metal jug. Secure the lid in place. Select the chunky function and leave to cook. Meanwhile cook the spaghetti (see step 5 above). Blend the soup to the consistency you prefer. Season to taste, if necessary. Serve the soup as in step 6 above.

Fruits

There is something surprising and unexpected about fruit soups. Although they are popular in some parts of the world, there's a lot to discover about them, and exciting new experiences lie in wait for you if you set out on the voyage. Fruits are vibrant, colourful superfoods, and these recipes are designed to enhance and complement their natural sharpness or sweetness. Fruit soups can be hot or chilled, and can be served as breakfast, a snack or a dessert.

Chilled Cucumber, Blueberry and Almond Gazpacho

A sweet fruity version of gazpacho. Very refreshing with ginger adding a little heat.

SERVES 4-6
1 cucumber
5cm (2in) piece of fresh root ginger
450g (1lb) blueberries, fresh or frozen
150ml (¼ pint) unsweetened apple juice
400ml (14fl oz) water
70g (2½oz) chopped almonds
2 tsp lemon zest
Crushed ice, olive oil and freshly milled black pepper, to serve.

1 Cut the cucumber in half lengthways, scoop out the seeds and thinly slice. Coarsely grate the root ginger, gather together with your hand and squeeze the juice into a cup. Discard the pulp.
2 Put all the ingredients into the glass jar and cover with the lid. Set the timer to 15 minutes and the temperature to high. Stir to mix. Bring to the boil, reduce the heat to simmer and cook for the remaining time, using the stir button occasionally. Blend to the consistency you prefer.
3 Ladle or pour the soup into a large bowl, leave to cool and chill until cold. To serve, ladle into bowls and top each with a little crushed ice, a drizzle of olive oil and a little black pepper.

JUG-STYLE SOUP MAKER
Thaw the blueberries, if frozen. Put the prepared cucumber (step 1 above) and other ingredients, into the metal jug. Top up with unsweetened apple juice or water if the level is below the minimum mark. Secure the lid in place. Select the chunky function and leave to cook. Use the blend button if necessary. Serve the soup as in step 3 above.

Plum and Coconut Soup

A lovely, delicately perfumed soup. This would be good
made with nectarines or greengages as well.

SERVES 4-6
650g (1lb 7oz) ripe plums
2 tsp cornflour
425ml (¾ pint) coconut milk
300ml (½ pint) water
1 tbsp clear honey
1 tsp lemon juice
Toasted coconut, to serve

1   Halve the plums and remove the stones. Cut into small pieces.
    Put the cornflour into a small cup and stir in 2–3 tablespoons of
    the coconut milk or water until blended.
2   Put all the ingredients into the glass jar and cover with the lid.
    Set the timer to 20 minutes and the temperature to high. Stir to
    mix. Bring to the boil, reduce the heat to simmer and cook for
    the remaining time, using the stir button occasionally. Blend to
    the consistency you prefer. Sweeten to taste with extra honey.
3   Ladle or pour the hot soup into bowls and scatter over a little
    toasted coconut. Serve immediately.

JUG-STYLE SOUP MAKER
Put the prepared plums (step 1 above) and other ingredients into the
metal jug. Top up with unsweetened grape juice or water if the level
is below the minimum mark. Secure the lid in place. Select the purée
function and leave to cook. If preferred, sweeten to taste with extra
honey. Serve the soup as in step 3 above.

Cherry and Chocolate Soup

Yes, chocolate is a superfood, too!

SERVES 4–6

140g (5oz) good quality dark chocolate with cocoa
solids above 70%
650g (1lb 7oz) pitted cherries, fresh or frozen
600ml (1 pint) unsweetened red grape juice
150ml (¼ pint) water
2 tsp sugar
2–3 drops vanilla extract
Crème fraîche, to serve

1   Coarsely grate the chocolate and put to one side for later. Cut
    each of the cherries in half.
2   Put all the ingredients, except the grated chocolate into the glass
    jar and cover with the lid. Set the timer to 20 minutes and the
    temperature to high. Stir to mix. Bring to the boil, reduce the
    heat to simmer and cook for the remaining time, using the stir
    button occasionally. Blend to the consistency you prefer.
3   Ladle or pour the hot soup into bowls. Swirl some grated
    chocolate into each bowl and top with a spoonful of crème
    fraîche. Serve immediately.

JUG-STYLE SOUP MAKER
Thaw the cherries, if frozen. Put the prepared cherries (step 1 above)
and other ingredients except the grated chocolate, into the metal jug.
Top up with unsweetened grape juice or water if the level is below
the minimum mark. Secure the lid in place. Select the purée function
and leave to cook. Serve the soup as in step 3 above.

Pomegranate and Grape Soup

Choose sweet, seedless grapes packed with lots of flavour.

SERVES 4-6

Large bunch of small, seedless black grapes, about 650g (1lb 7oz)

425ml (¾ pint) unsweetened pomegranate juice

300ml (½ pint) water

2 tsp orange zest

Pomegranate seeds and Greek yogurt, to serve

1. Pull the grapes from the stalks and cut each in half.
2. Put all the ingredients into the glass jar and cover with the lid. Set the timer to 15 minutes and the temperature to high. Stir to mix. Bring to the boil, reduce the heat to simmer and cook for the remaining time, using the stir button occasionally. Blend to the consistency you prefer.
3. Ladle or pour the hot soup into bowls. Top each bowl with a scattering of pomegranate seeds and a swirl of yogurt and serve immediately.

JUG-STYLE SOUP MAKER

Put all the prepared ingredients (step 1 above) and other ingredients into the metal jug. Top up with unsweetened pomegranate juice or water if the level is below the minimum mark. Secure the lid in place. Select the chunky function and leave to cook. Use the blend button if necessary. Serve the soup as in step 3 above.

Cranberry and Pear Soup

Try this soup with apple or melon instead of the pear, when you feel like a change.

SERVES 4–6
4 ripe pears
1 orange
350g (12oz) cranberries, fresh or frozen
300ml (½ pint) unsweetened red grape juice
450ml (16fl oz) water
2 tbsp clear honey
Few drops vanilla extract
Crème fraîche, to serve

1   Peel, core and finely chop the pears. Finely grate or zest half the orange to give about 2 teaspoons. Cut the orange in half and squeeze out the juice.
2   Put all the ingredients into the glass jar and cover with the lid. Set the timer to 20 minutes and the temperature to high. Stir to mix. Bring to the boil, reduce the heat to simmer and cook for the remaining time, using the stir button occasionally. Blend to the consistency you prefer.
3   Ladle or pour the hot soup into bowls. Top each bowl with a swirl of crème fraîche and serve immediately.

JUG-STYLE SOUP MAKER
Thaw the cranberries, if frozen. Put all the prepared ingredients (step 1 above) and other ingredients into the metal jug. Top up with unsweetened grape juice or water if the level is below the minimum mark. Secure the lid in place. Select the chunky function and leave to cook. Use the blend button if necessary. Serve the soup as in step 3 above.

Blueberry and Melon Soup

Choose a ripe sweet melon for added natural sweetness.

SERVES 4-6
1 melon wedge, to give about 250g (9oz) flesh
450g (1lb) blueberries, fresh or frozen
300ml (½ pint) unsweetened white grape juice
450ml (16fl oz) water
Pinch of ground cinnamon
A few mint leaves and natural yogurt, to serve

1 Discard any melon seeds. Scoop out the flesh and roughly cut
   into small cubes, about 2.5cm (1in).
2 Put all the ingredients into the glass jar and cover with the lid.
   Set the timer to 15 minutes and the temperature to high. Stir to
   mix. Bring to the boil, reduce the heat to simmer and cook for
   the remaining time using the stir button occasionally. Blend to
   the consistency you prefer.
3 Ladle or pour the hot soup into bowls. Top with a spoonful of
   natural yogurt and mint leaves. Serve immediately.

JUG-STYLE SOUP MAKER
Thaw the blueberries, if frozen. Put the prepared melon (step 1
above) and other ingredients, into the metal jug. Top up with
unsweetened grape juice or water if the level is below the minimum
mark. Secure the lid in place. Select the chunky function and leave to
cook. Use the blend button if necessary. Serve the soup as in step 3
above.

Orange, Grapefruit and Lime Soup

A very citrus soup. Use blood oranges for extra colour.

SERVES 4-6
5 sweet oranges
2 limes
1 grapefruit
4 mint leaves
300ml (½ pint) unsweetened apple juice
450ml (16fl oz) water
2 tbsp sugar or clear honey
Mint leaves and toasted chopped hazelnuts, to serve

1   Finely grate or zest the rind of one of the oranges. Peel the rind and pith from the oranges, limes and grapefruit. With a sharp knife, remove the fruit segments and cut each segment in half. Tear the mint leaves in half.
2   Put all the ingredients into the glass jar and cover with the lid. Set the timer to 20 minutes and the temperature to high. Stir to mix. Bring to the boil, reduce the heat to simmer and cook for the remaining time, using the stir button occasionally. Blend to the consistency you prefer.
3   If preferred, sweeten to taste with extra honey. Ladle or pour the hot soup into bowls. Top each bowl with mint leaves and a few chopped hazelnuts. Serve immediately.

JUG-STYLE SOUP MAKER
Put all the prepared ingredients (step 1 above) and other ingredients into the metal jug. Top up with unsweetened apple juice or water if the level is below the minimum mark. Secure the lid in place. Select the purée function and leave to cook. If preferred, sweeten to taste with a little sugar or clear honey and serve the soup as in step 3 above.

Mixed Berry Soup

This soup is perfect to make when there is a glut of fruit around in late summer.

SERVES 4-6
2 tsp cornflour
300g (10½oz) blackberries, fresh or frozen
200g (7oz) raspberries, fresh or frozen
200g (7oz) blueberries, fresh or frozen
1 tsp cornflour
300ml (½ pint) unsweetened green grape juice
1 tbsp soft brown sugar or clear honey
400ml (14fl oz) water
1 tsp lemon juice
Single cream or natural yogurt, to serve

1   Put the cornflour into a small cup and stir in 2–3 tablespoons of the grape juice or water until blended to a paste.
2   Put all the ingredients into the glass jar and cover with the lid. Set the timer to 15 minutes and the temperature to high. Stir to mix. Bring to the boil, reduce the heat to simmer and cook for the remaining time, using the stir button occasionally. Blend to the consistency you prefer.
3   Ladle or pour the hot soup into bowls. Top each bowl with a swirl of cream or yogurt and serve immediately.

JUG-STYLE SOUP MAKER
Thaw the berries, if frozen. Put all the prepared ingredients (step 1 above) and other ingredients into the metal jug. Top up with unsweetened grape juice or water if the level is below the minimum mark. Secure the lid in place. Select the chunky function and leave to cook. Use the blend button for a few seconds. Serve the soup as in step 3 above.

Peach and Redcurrant Soup with Rice

A refreshing soup with a vibrant colour.

SERVES 4-6
250g (9oz) redcurrants, fresh or frozen
5 ripe peaches
1 tsp cornflour
2 tsp soft brown sugar or clear honey
300ml (½ pint) unsweetened apple juice
400ml (14fl oz) water
100g (3½oz) uncooked rice or pearled spelt
Toasted flaked almonds, to serve

1   Use a fork to strip the redcurrants from their stalks. Halve the peaches and remove the stones. Cut into small pieces.
2   Put all the ingredients, except the rice or pearled spelt into the glass jar and cover with the lid. Set the timer to 20 minutes and the temperature to high. Stir to mix. Bring to the boil, reduce the heat to simmer and cook for the remaining time, using the stir button occasionally. Blend to the consistency you prefer.
3   Meanwhile, cook the rice or spelt according to the packet instructions.
4   Spoon the piping hot cooked rice or spelt into hot soup bowls and ladle or pour the hot soup over.
5   Top each bowl with a few toasted flaked almonds and serve immediately.

JUG-STYLE SOUP MAKER
Thaw the redcurrants, if frozen. Put all the prepared ingredients except the rice or pearled spelt (step 1 above) and other ingredients into the metal jug. Top up with unsweetened apple juice or water if the level is below the minimum mark. Secure the lid in place. Select the chunky function and leave to cook. Use the blend button for a few seconds. Cook the rice or spelt (step 3 above). Serve the soup as in steps 4 and 5 above.

Dried Fruit and Apple Soup

This is an easy soup, made mostly from store-cupboard ingredients.

SERVES 4-6

1 Bramley cooking apple, about 250g (9oz)
280g (10oz) ready-to-eat dried fruits such as mango strips,
   pineapple, apricots or pears
5cm (2in) piece of fresh root ginger
300ml (½ pint) unsweetened apple juice
450ml (16fl oz) water
¼ tsp ground cinnamon
Thick natural yogurt, to serve

1   Peel, core and roughly chop the apple. Finely chop the dried
    fruits. Coarsely grate the root ginger, gather together with your
    hand and squeeze the juice into a cup. Discard the pulp.
2   Put all the ingredients into the glass jar and cover with the lid.
    Set the timer to 30 minutes and the temperature to high. Stir to
    mix. Bring to the boil, reduce the heat to simmer and cook for
    the remaining time, using the stir button occasionally. Blend to
    the consistency you prefer.
3   Ladle or pour the hot soup into bowls. Top each bowl with a
    spoonful of yogurt and serve immediately.

JUG-STYLE SOUP MAKER

Put all the prepared ingredients (step 1 above) and other ingredients
into the metal jug. Top up with unsweetened apple juice or water if
the level is below the minimum mark. Secure the lid in place. Select
the purée function and leave to cook. Serve the soup as in step 3
above.

Essential Extras

For vegetable, fish and meat soups to be successful, you need to have a really good stock. It's nice to make your own. Follow any of these stock recipes – there are five to choose from – and you'll be pleased with the results. Also included here are some useful extras, like the crushed walnut pesto and the spicy red pepper relish which can be stirred into soups or used in other ways, and the herby oat bread and mini seeded spelt flatbreads to accompany soups when you're hungry or to make a main meal.

Herby Oat Bread

In place of the buttermilk you could use half water and half plain yogurt, or milk with a little lemon juice added.

MAKES ONE LOAF

300g (10½oz) unbleached strong white flour,
    plus extra for dusting
½ tsp fine sea salt
1 x 7g sachet fast-action dried yeast
1 tsp sugar
150g (5½oz) whole rolled oats, plus extra for topping
1 tsp dried mixed herbs
2 tsp olive oil
150ml (¼ pint) buttermilk
200ml (7fl oz) lukewarm water

TOPPING

Milk or water for brushing
Small amount of whole rolled oats

1   Sift the flour and salt into a large mixing bowl. Stir in the yeast, sugar, oats and herbs.
2   Mix in the oil, buttermilk and enough of the water to give a soft dough.
3   Gather the dough into a ball and turn out onto a lightly dusted surface. Knead for about 10 minutes until smooth and elastic.
4   Press and shape the dough into a round, about 18cm (7in) diameter and place on a greased baking sheet. Cut four slashes along the top of the dough and cover loosely with oiled cling film. Leave to prove until doubled in size, about 40 minutes.
5   Meanwhile preheat the oven to 190°C, fan 170°C, gas 5.
6   Remove the cling film. Brush the top of the dough with milk or water and sprinkle over a few rolled oats.
7   Put into the hot oven and cook for 30–40 minutes, until the loaf sounds hollow when tapped underneath.

Mini Seeded Spelt Flatbreads

Spelt flour is made from an ancient grain and has a delicious nutty taste. These flatbreads don't have to be perfectly shaped – rustic is better.

MAKES 12-14 FLATBREADS

500g (1lb 2oz) spelt flour, plus extra for dusting

½ tsp fine sea salt

1 x 7g sachet fast-action dried yeast

1 tsp clear honey

350ml (12fl oz) lukewarm water

TOPPING

Beaten egg or milk, for brushing

3–4 tbsp mixed seeds, such as sesame, poppy, linseed or chia.

1   Sift the flour and salt into a large mixing bowl. Stir in the yeast and honey.
2   Mix in enough of the water to give a soft dough.
3   Gather the dough into a ball and turn out onto a lightly dusted surface. Knead for about 10 minutes until smooth and elastic.
4   Divide the dough into 12–14 pieces and roughly shape each one into a ball. Cover loosely with oiled cling film. Leave to prove until doubled in size, about 20–30 minutes.
5   Meanwhile preheat the oven to 220°C, fan 200°C, gas 7.
6   With a floured rolling pin or just using your fingers, roll or pull the dough into ovals or rounds.
7   Arrange on greased baking sheets. Brush the tops of the flatbreads with a little beaten egg or milk and sprinkle over the seeds.
8   Put into the hot oven and cook for about 10–15 minutes until golden.

FOR BREAD ROLLS

If you prefer to make bread rolls, divide the dough into 8 pieces. Shape each piece into a ball. Prove as in step 4 and bake in the hot oven for 15–20 minutes.

Vegetable Stock

Use whichever vegetables are in season, you don't have to choose the ones listed here. They don't have to be peeled, just washed thoroughly.

MAKES ABOUT 1 LITRE (1¾ PINTS)
1 small lemon
1 onion
1 potato
2 carrots
2 celery sticks
1 leek
6 black peppercorns
1 bay leaf
4 sprigs of parsley
3 or 4 sprigs of fresh herbs such as fennel, thyme or rosemary

1   Roughly chop the lemon, onion and potato. Roughly slice the carrots, celery sticks and leek.
2   Put all the ingredients into a large saucepan and pour over 1 litre (1¾ pints) cold water.
3   Bring to the boil and remove any scum that rises to the surface with a slotted spoon.
4   Lower the heat, partially cover with a lid and cook for 40 minutes, occasionally removing any scum.
5   Strain the stock through a fine-meshed sieve.
6   Use at once or leave to cool and chill for up to two days or freeze.

For a more concentrated flavour pour the stock into a saucepan. Bring to the boil, reduce the heat and simmer until reduced by half.

Mushroom Stock

Mushrooms make a very earthy tasting stock which packs a punch. I often add two or three dried mushrooms.

MAKES ABOUT 1 LITRE (1¾ PINTS)
450g (1lb) mixed mushrooms
3 shallots
2 red peppers
2 celery sticks
2 garlic cloves
1 small lemon
3 tbsp sunflower oil
6 black peppercorns
1 tbsp wholegrain mustard
3 sprigs of thyme
Small handful of parsley stalks

1   Slice the mushrooms and shallots. Cut the red peppers in half, remove the stalks and seeds and roughly chop. Slice the celery sticks, garlic and lemon.
2   Heat the oil in a large saucepan and add the prepared ingredients. Cook for 5–10 minutes, until beginning to brown and soften.
3   Add the remaining ingredients to the saucepan and pour over 1 litre (1¾ pints) cold water.
4   Bring to the boil and remove any scum that rises to the surface with a slotted spoon.
5   Lower the heat, partially cover with a lid and cook for 40 minutes, occasionally removing any scum.
6   Strain the stock through a fine-meshed sieve.
7   Use at once or leave to cool and chill for up to two days or freeze.

For a more concentrated flavour pour the stock into a saucepan. Bring to the boil, reduce the heat and simmer until reduced by half.

Fish Stock

Use salmon or white fish bones, as oily fish gives an unpleasant flavour to the stock. For the best flavour don't cook the stock for too long.

MAKES ABOUT 1 LITRE (1¾ PINTS)
1 kg (2¼lb) salmon or white fish bones, heads and trimmings
1 small lemon
1 onion
1 carrot
2 celery sticks
150ml (¼ pint) dry white wine or water
1 fennel sprig
6 black peppercorns
1 bay leaf
2 sprigs of thyme
6 sprigs of parsley
6 sprigs of fennel

1 Cut any large pieces of fish with a knife to fit your pan. Roughly chop the lemon, onion and carrot and slice the celery stalks.
2 Put all the ingredients into a large saucepan and pour over 1 litre (1¾ pints) cold water.
3 Bring to the boil and remove any scum that rises to the surface with a slotted spoon.
4 Lower the heat, partially cover with a lid and cook for 20 minutes, occasionally removing any scum.
5 Strain the stock through a fine-meshed sieve.
6 Use at once or leave to cool and chill for up to two days or freeze.

Poultry or Game Stock

Raw bones give the best flavour, but cooked carcasses do make good stock.

MAKES ABOUT 1 LITRE (1¾ PINTS)
1 kg (2¼lb) raw or cooked poultry or game carcasses
1 onion
1 carrot
2 celery sticks
3 garlic cloves, unpeeled
1 bay leaf
6 black peppercorns
6 juniper berries (if making game stock)
3 or 4 sprigs of thyme

1   Cut or break the poultry or game into pieces. Roughly chop the onion and carrot and slice the celery sticks.
2   Put all the ingredients – including the juniper berries if making a game stock – into a large saucepan and pour over 1 litre (1¾ pints) cold water.
3   Bring to the boil and remove any scum that rises to the surface with a slotted spoon.
4   Lower the heat, partially cover with a lid and cook for 2–3 hours, occasionally removing any scum.
5   Strain the stock through a fine-meshed sieve.
6   Use at once or leave to cool and chill for up to two days or freeze.

For a more concentrated flavour pour the stock into a saucepan. Bring to the boil, reduce the heat and simmer until reduced by half.

Meat Stock

Browning the bones in a hot oven gives a richer, darker stock.

MAKES ABOUT 1.3 LITRE (2¼ PINTS)

2 onions

2 carrots

2 celery sticks

1kg (2¼lb) raw meat bones: beef, lamb, pork, ham or oxtail

3 tomatoes

3 garlic cloves, unpeeled

2 bay leaves

10 black peppercorns

2 sprigs of parsley

3 sprigs of thyme

1   Preheat the oven to 200°C, fan 185°C, gas 6.
2   Roughly chop the onions and carrots and slice the celery sticks.
3   Place the prepared vegetables and the meat bones in a roasting dish and put into the hot oven. Cook for 30–40 minutes, turning the ingredients occasionally until browned.
4   With a slotted spoon, lift the roasted bones and vegetables into a large saucepan. Drain off any fat in the roasting dish and scrape any sediment into the saucepan.
5   Add the remaining ingredients to the saucepan and pour over 2 litres (3½ pints) cold water.
6   Bring to the boil and remove any scum that rises to the surface with a slotted spoon.
7   Lower the heat, partially cover with a lid and cook for 2–3 hours, occasionally removing any scum.
8   Strain the stock through a fine-meshed sieve and skim off any surface fat.
9   Use at once or leave to cool and chill for up to two days or freeze.

For a more concentrated flavour pour the stock into a saucepan. Bring to the boil, reduce the heat and simmer until reduced by half.

Crushed Walnut Pesto

A little pesto stirred into a bowl of soup adds colour and flavour. It is delicious made with toasted almonds and parsley.

SERVES 6–8
70g (2½oz) walnut pieces, about a small handful
A large bunch of basil
2 garlic cloves
60g (2¼oz) Parmesan or pecorino cheese
250ml (9fl oz) extra virgin olive oil, plus extra
Freshly ground black pepper

1 Heat a frying pan and dry-fry the walnuts for a minute or two until lightly toasted. Keep turning them in the heat, being careful not to let them burn. Tip them onto a plate and leave until cold.
2 Pull the leaves from the basil stalks and roughly chop the garlic clove. Grate the Parmesan or pecorino cheese.
3 Put all the ingredients into a food processor and whizz the ingredients together, or if you've time, use a mortar and pestle. If necessary, add a little more oil to give a soft paste. Season to taste.
4 Spoon the pesto into a small bowl and cover the surface with a little extra oil. Store in the fridge for up to two weeks.

Spicy Red Pepper Relish

A fresh tasting relish is somewhere between a chutney and a pickle. Stir into soups or mix with a little grated cheese, spread on toasted bread and pop under the grill until golden. Cut into small pieces and use as croûtons.

MAKES ABOUT 900G (2LB)
4 large red peppers
2 red chillies
2 green apples
2 medium red onions
2 garlic cloves
300ml (½ pint) red wine vinegar
300ml (½ pint) water
140g (5oz) soft brown sugar

1 Cut the peppers and chillies in half, remove and discard the seeds and stalks, and finely chop. Cut the apples in half, leaving the skin on and cut the fruit into small pieces. Finely chop the onions and garlic.
2 Pour the vinegar, water and sugar into a large saucepan. Heat gently until the sugar has dissolved.
3 Stir in the prepared ingredients and bring to the boil. Reduce the temperature and simmer for 25 minutes, stirring occasionally. If you prefer a smooth relish, whizz with a stick blender.
4 Stir well before spooning into warm sterilised jars and sealing. Keep refrigerated. Use within four weeks.

Index